THE WORLD BIBLIOGRAPHICAL SERIES

This series, which is principally designed for the English speaker, will eventually cover every country in the world, each in a separate volume comprising annotated entries on works dealing with its history, geography, economy and politics; and with its people, their culture, customs, religion and social organization. Attention will also be paid to current living conditions – housing, education, newspapers, clothing, etc. – that are all too often ignored in standard bibliographies; and to those particular aspects relevant to individual countries. Each volume seeks to achieve, by use of careful selectivity and critical assessment of the literature, an expression of the country and an appreciation of its nature and national aspirations, to guide the reader towards an understanding of its importance. The keynote of the series is to provide, in a uniform format, an interpretation of each country that will express its culture, its place in the world, and the qualities and background that make it unique. The views expressed in individual volumes, however, are not necessarily those of the publisher.

VOLUMES IN THE SERIES

Bhutan

WORLD BIBLIOGRAPHICAL SERIES

General Editors:
Robert G. Neville (Executive Editor)
John J. Horton

Robert A. Myers   Ian Wallace
Hans H. Wellisch   Ralph Lee Woodward, Jr.

John J. Horton is Deputy Librarian of the University of Bradford and currently Chairman of its Academic Board of Studies in Social Sciences. He has maintained a longstanding interest in the discipline of area studies and its associated bibliographical problems, with special reference to European Studies. In particular he has published in the field of Icelandic and of Yugoslav studies, including the two relevant volumes in the World Bibliographical Series.

Robert A. Myers is Associate Professor of Anthropology in the Division of Social Sciences and Director of Study Abroad Programs at Alfred University, Alfred, New York. He has studied post-colonial island nations of the Caribbean and has spent two years in Nigeria on a Fulbright Lectureship. His interests include international public health, historical anthropology and developing societies. In addition to *Amerindians of the Lesser Antilles: a bibliography* (1981), *A Resource Guide to Dominica, 1493–1986* (1987) and numerous articles, he has compiled the World Bibliographical Series volumes on *Dominica* (1987) and *Nigeria* (1989).

Ian Wallace is Professor of Modern Languages at Loughborough University of Technology. A graduate of Oxford in French and German, he also studied in Tübingen, Heidelberg and Lausanne before taking teaching posts at universities in the USA, Scotland and England. He specializes in East German affairs, especially literature and culture, on which he has published numerous articles and books. In 1979 he founded the journal *GDR Monitor*, which he continues to edit.

Hans H. Wellisch is Professor emeritus at the College of Library and Information Services, University of Maryland. He was President of the American Society of Indexers and was a member of the International Federation for Documentation. He is the author of numerous articles and several books on indexing and abstracting, and has published *The Conversion of Scripts* and *Indexing and Abstracting: an International Bibliography*. He also contributes frequently to *Journal of the American Society for Information Science, The Indexer* and other professional journals.

Ralph Lee Woodward, Jr. is Chairman of the Department of History at Tulane University, New Orleans, where he has been Professor of History since 1970. He is the author of *Central America, a Nation Divided*, 2nd ed. (1985), as well as several monographs and more than sixty scholarly articles on modern Latin America. He has also compiled volumes in the World Bibliographical Series on *Belize* (1980), *Nicaragua* (1983), and *El Salvador* (1988). Dr. Woodward edited the Central American section of the *Research Guide to Central America and the Caribbean* (1985) and is currently editor of the Central American history section of the *Handbook of Latin American Studies*.

VOLUME 116

Bhutan

Ramesh C. Dogra

Compiler

CLIO PRESS

OXFORD, ENGLAND · SANTA BARBARA, CALIFORNIA
DENVER, COLORADO

British Library Cataloguing in Publication Data

Dogra, Ramesh C. (Ramesh Chander) 1936–
Bhutan – (World bibliographical series; v.116).
1. Bhutan. Bibliographies
I. Title   II. Series 016.95498

ISBN 1–85109–128–9

Clio Press Ltd.,
55 St. Thomas' Street,
Oxford OX1 1JG, England.

ABC-CLIO,
130 Cremona Drive,
Santa Barbara,
CA 93117, USA.

Designed by Bernard Crossland.
Typeset by Columns Design and Production Services Ltd., Reading, England.
Printed and bound in Great Britain by
Billing and Sons Ltd., Worcester.

954.98'00169.

Dedicated
to
Mr K. L. Sharma – an illustrious scholar and a pioneer in
the field of Indian journalism
and
Mrs S. Sharma who believes in the glory of reason, the
richness of humanism and the ecstasy of duty.

Contents

Contents

Introduction

Bhutan and its peoples

Bhutan is a small kingdom in the eastern Himalaya, strategically located between India and Tibet (now a part of China). It is bounded on the north by Tibet; on the east by the Tawang country, a narrow outlying dependency of Tibet which stretches southwards to the confines of Assam; on the south by Gauhati and Goalpara districts; and on the west by the Chumbi Valley, Gangtok district of Sikkim, and the Darjeeling district of West Bengal. Bhutan stretches 190 miles from east to west and 90 miles from north to south. Its area is about 18,000 square miles (46,600 sq. km), and in 1988 its population was estimated at approximately 1,400,000. Of these, Hindus, of Nepalese origin, form 25 to 30 per cent. Life expectancy in 1985 was 48 years. The capital is at Thimphu with a population, in 1987, of 15,000.

The lofty peaks and ranges of the Himalayas extend along the whole of the northern boundary of Bhutan, and great spurs stretch southwards from the main chain along its eastern and western boundaries. Within these mighty natural barriers is a succession of hill ranges, the general direction of which in western Bhutan is from north-west to south-east and in eastern Bhutan from north-east to south-west. The Dongkya range is the tri-junction point of the Sikkim–Bhutan–Tibet boundary. From Chumalhari, on the Tibetan boundary at the north-west corner of Bhutan, another ridge strikes southwards to form the boundary between Jalpaiguri district of West Bengal and Bhutan. Farther east very little is known about the main chain, but it has been ascertained that its chief offshoots trend southwards: these include the Black mountain range, with ramifications south-west and south-east in the Tongsa division. This mountainous region sends out numerous rivers in a more or less southerly direction, all of which eventually find their way into the Brahmaputra. Their courses in Bhutan are confined between high rocky mountains, and since the gradients of their beds fall steeply, they become furious

Introduction

torrents in the rains, and hardly any of them are fordable. Proceeding
from west to east, the chief rivers are the Di-chu, Amo-chu or Torsa,
Chin-chu, Ma-chu, Mati-chu, and Dangme-chu. The lower mountain
ranges are composed chiefly of a coarse, decomposing granite
sandstone, while gneiss, hornblendic slate, micaceous slate, and
brown and ochre-coloured sandstones form the boulders in the beds
of the streams. At an elevation of 8,000 or 9,000 feet, a talcose slate
has been observed, containing many garnets, and in some cases
threaded with large grains of titaniferous iron ore.

Above 5,000 feet the mountain slopes are generally covered with
forest with many varieties of stately trees, including the beech, ash,
birch, maple, cypress, and yew. At an elevation of 8,000 to 9,000 feet
is a zone of vegetation consisting principally of oaks and rhodo-
dendrons, and above this again is a profusion of firs and pines. The
lower ranges of the hills teem with animal life. Tigers are not
common, except near the river Tista, but elephants are so numerous
that they are a danger to travellers. Leopards are found in the valleys
and deer may be seen almost anywhere: the musk deer in the snows,
and the barking deer on every hillside. Wild hog live higher up, and
bears and rhinoceros are also found. Large squirrels are common,
along with pheasants, partridges, jungle-fowl, pigeons, and other
small game.

The climate of Bhutan varies with the altitude. The mountainous
north is as cold as Siberia, with perpetual snow on the summits, but
the centre has a more moderate climate, though the winters are cold.
The inhabitants of Punakha are afraid of exposing themselves to the
blazing sun, and those in Gasa experience all the rigours of winter
and are chilled by perpetual snows: yet these two places are within
sight of each other. The rainfall in central Bhutan is about 40 inches
(1,000 mm); in the south it approaches 200 inches (5,000 mm).

Broadly speaking, the Bhutanese people are composed of three
different racial elements: the Mongloid and the Indo-Aryans of
Assam and upper Burma. The majority of the people in Bhutan are
called Bhutias. They are of Tibetan descent and are also known as
the Dragon people (Drukpas). Hindus of Nepali origin form 25 to 30
per cent of the population of Bhutan, while some small communities
in eastern Bhutan appear to be related to the hill tribes of Assam.
Bhutia migrated to Bhutan between the fourteenth and the
seventeenth centuries, but some migrated more recently. Bhutias are
at home amongst their cattle and mules, and physically they are a fine
race, hardy and vigorous. Nepali Hindus migrated to western Bhutan
on the Indian border during the late nineteenth and early twentieth
centuries. The reasons which induced the Nepalese to migrate into
western Bhutan included the plentiful supply of land, and the absence

of any restrictions on taking it up and clearing it.

The economy is mostly agrarian. In 1985, about 95 per cent of the economically active population was engaged in agriculture, forestry and fishing, although only about 9 per cent of the land was under cultivation. Forests cover some 70 per cent of the country and a forest-based industrial complex has begun at Gedu, while a plant for the production of particle board was constructed in 1983. The chief crops are rice, corn, wheat, millet, barley, mustard, vegetables, walnuts, oranges, and the spice cardomom. Some farms also raise yaks, cattle, sheep, pigs, and ponies which are very useful for mountain transportation. The common small-scale industries are the weaving of cloth, basket- and mat-making, paper-making, and hand-work in wood, leather, and metal.

For administrative purposes, the country is divided into eighteen districts (Dzongkhags). The name and population of these districts in mid-1985 was as follows: Bumthang, with a population of 23,842; Chirang, 108,807; Dagana, 28,352; Gasa, 16,907; Gaylephug, 111,283; Haa, 16,715; Lhuntshi, 39,635; Mongar, 73,239; Paro, 46,615; Pema Gatshel, 37,141; Punakha, 16,700; Samchi, 172,109; Samdrup Jongkhar, 73,044; Shemgang, 44,516; Tashigang, 177,718; Thimphu, 58,660; Tongsa, 26,017; and Wangdiphodrang, 47,152. Each district in Bhutan is headed by a chief administrator (Dzongda) and a person in charge of judicial matters (Thrimpon). Dzongdas are appointed by the Royal Civil Service Commission, established in 1982, but previously they were appointed by the King. The principal officers under the Dzongda are the Dzongda Wongma and the Dzongrab, and they are responsible for local administration in each district. The lowest adminstrative unit in all districts is the bloc (gewog) of several villages.

The linguistic situation of Bhutan is complex as there are many dialects. The most important of these are Ngalonggikha of western Bhutan, Tsangla or Sharchopikha of eastern Bhutan, Bumthangpikha of central Bhutan, Kurteypikha of north-eastern Bhutan, Khenkha of central-south Bhutan and Nepali of southern Bhutan. Dzongkha, the official language is spoken in western and northern Bhutan, and English is taught in all schools. All these dialects are related to the Tibetan language and are written in the Tibetan script. The Nepali language is written in Devanagari script and comes from the family of Indo-Aryan languages. Dzongkha is spoken by a large number of people, and is the main medium of communication. Bhutan Broadcasting Service, Thimphu, broadcasts a daily programme in English, Sharchopikha, Dzongkha and Nepali.

The introduction of written script in Bhutan is closely related to the spread of Buddhism during the 8th century AD by Padma Sambhava (known as Guru Rimpoche in Bhutan). He taught Mahayana Buddhism to the King of Bumthang and his people, and also taught them how to read and write in Bhutanese script which is slightly different from the Tibetan script. In the first half of the ninth century AD, the standard classical Tibetan was fixed and it became the religious language (Choekay) for all the Buddhists living in Tibet, Mongolia, Bhutan, Sikkim and other Himalayan states. There are various dialects of Tibetan spoken in the western, eastern, central and north-eastern Bhutan, but the main reason for adopting Dzongkha as the national language was that it maintains the basic standard set by Choekay and lends itself readily to written standardization.

Free education is available, but the government schools cannot accommodate all children. Primary education starts at the age of seven, and secondary education starts at twelve for a further period of five years. All the schools are co-educational and follow a British pattern of education. There are no private or missionary schools, but every school is subsidized by the government and English is taught in all of them. Social welfare is a new thing in Bhutan, but in 1984 the country had 25 hospitals and some local dispensaries providing minimum medical care.

Bhutan opened its door to tourism in 1974, and some hotels and transport facilities were provided. Wildlife sanctuaries have also been established. The government's policy is to limit the number of tourists. They come mainly from Europe, Japan and the USA, and may visit the country individually or by package or trekking tours.

A modern postal system was introduced in the country in 1962. There are 56 general post offices and 30 branch post offices. In 1986 there were 943 km of telephone lines, 13 automatic exchanges and 1,945 telephones. An international microwave link connects Thimphu to the Calcutta and Delhi satellite connections. Thimphu and Phuntsholing are also connected by telex to Delhi. The Bank of Bhutan was established in 1968, and has 32 branches throughout the country. The Royal Monetary Authority was founded in 1982 at Thimphu to act as Bhutan's central bank.

Historical survey

The origin of the present name Bhutan remains obscure. It is presumed that it was derived from the Indian term Bhotanta which means the end of Tibetan boundary. There are also three other traditional names of Bhutan: Lon-Mon Khashi (the southern Mon country of four approaches); Lho-Mon Tsenden Jong (the southern Mon country of sandalwood); and Lho Jong Menjong (the southern country of medicinal herbs). Mon is a general term which means all non-Tibetan and non-Indian people in the Himalayas.

The early history of Bhutan is buried in an almost impenetrable obscurity. The number of stone stools and megaliths found in the country suggest that Bhutan was populated around 2000 to 1500 BC, but it is difficult to draw any conclusions from this since no archaeological surveys have been conducted. However, the country was formerly occupied by a tribe called Bhotias Tephu, who are believed to have been from the same race as the Kacharis and Cooch of the adjoining plains, and who were subjugated by a band of Tibetan soldiers. The soldiers settled in the country and intermarried with the natives, and from them have sprung the people now called Bhotias. The known history of Bhutan begins with the advent of Buddhism in the middle of the seventh century. The two oldest Buddhist temples (Jampa Lhakhang in Bumthang and the Kichu Lhakhang in Paro) were constructed at that time. The Buddhist religion has played a great part in shaping the course of Bhutan's history. About 1630 AD a refugee called Drukpa Lama from Tibet made himself the first Dharma Raja (Shabdung), with both spiritual and temporal powers. He made the Drukpa sect of Tibetan Buddhism the official religion, and appointed Dev Raja (temporal powers) and four provincial governors (Penlops) to assist him in the administration. Soon the country was administered by the Dharma Raja and Deva Raja, but they were little more than pawns in the struggle for power between the two most powerful Penlops in the country.

The relationship between the British and Bhutan commenced in 1772, when the Bhotias invaded the principality of Cooch Behar. The ruler of that state invoked British aid, and a force was dispatched to his assistance to expel the invaders. Peace was concluded in 1774 through the mediation of the Tashi Lama, then Regent of Tibet. In 1783 Captain Turner was deputed to Bhutan, with a view to promoting commercial intercourse, but his mission proved unsuccessful. From this period few dealings took place with Bhutan until the occupation of Assam by the British in 1826. It was then discovered that the Bhotias had usurped the strip of land along the foot of the mountains, called the Duars or passes. Captain Pemberton was deputed to Bhutan to adjust the points of difference, but his negotiations were fruitless. In 1863 the Hon. Ashley Eden was sent as an envoy to Bhutan, where he was subjected to the grossest insults and, under compulsion, signed a treaty surrendering the Duars to Bhutan and making many other concessions. On hearing this the Governor-General of India issued a proclamation dated 12 November 1864, annexing the western Duars, and the Bhutan Government was compelled to sue for a peace treaty. It was concluded on 11 November 1865. In the following year, all the eighteen Duars of East Bengal and Assam were formally ceded to India. As the revenue of Bhutan depended mainly on these Duars, the British India Government undertook to pay in return an allowance starting at Rs. 25,000 a year and rising in three years to a maximum of twice that amount. Since then relations with Bhutan have been almost uninterruptedly satisfactory. On the occasion of the Tibet Mission of 1904, the Bhotias gave strong proof of their friendly attitude; not only did they consent to the survey of a road through Bhutan to Chumbi Valley, but their ruler Ugyen Wangchuck, the Tongsa Penlop (Governor of Tongsa) accompanied the British troops to Lhasa, and assisted in the negotiations with the Tibetan authorities. For these services he was made a KCIE. At that time the struggle for power between two most powerful Penlops of Tongsa and Paro was going on, and the British sided with the Penlop of Tongsa (now Sir Ugyen Dorji Wangchuck) and established an absolute monarchy in Bhutan in 1907. On 17 December 1907 Sir Ugyen Wangchuck was unanimously elected hereditary King of Bhutan by an assembly consisting of representatives of the clergy, the government and the people. The Bhutanese title of a King was Druk Gyalpo, but from now onwards he was known as the King of Bhutan.

In January 1910 the British Government amended its treaty of 1865 and agreed that the British Government would not interfere in the internal affairs of Bhutan, and the Bhutan Government agreed to be guided by the advice of the British Government in regard to its external affairs. After the independence of India a fresh treaty was concluded with Bhutan; under that treaty Bhutan continues to be guided by the Government of India in regard to its external relations, while the Government of India have undertaken not to interfere in the internal affairs of Bhutan.

Ugyen Wangchuck died in 1926 and was succeeded by his son Jigme Wangchuck who reigned over the country until his death in 1952. The reign of the third King Jigme Dorji Wangchuck (1952-72) was marked by progress and opening the country to the outside world. From October 1969 the absolute monarchy was changed to a modified form of constitutional monarchy. There is no formal constitution, but the written rules (which are changed periodically) govern procedures for the election of members of the Royal Advisory Council (Lodoi Tsokde) and the Legislature/National Assembly (Tshogdu), and define the duties and powers of those bodies. The National Assembly, established in 1952, has 151 members and meets twice a year, in spring and autumn. Two-thirds are representatives of the people and they are directly elected by the people for a three-year term. All Bhutanese over 25 years may be candidates. Ten seats are reserved for religious bodies, while the remaining members are nominated by the King; those include government officials, the ministers and members of the Royal Advisory Council, The Assembly enacts laws and advises the King on constitutional and political matters; the Royal Advisory Council, established in 1965, comprises 10 members: one nominee of the King, two monks representing the state religion, six people's representatives and a Chairman (Kalyon), also nominated by the King. The people's representatives have their names endorsed at the village assemblies. The Council's principal task is to advise the King, as head of government, and to supervise all aspects of administration. The Royal Advisory Council is a sort of permanent government department and it is in permanent session. Its members serve for five years and may be re-elected.

The country made great progress during the reign of the third King. In 1963 Bhutan joined the Colombo Plan and in 1971 it became a member of the United Nations (UNO). The restructuring of the country's social, economic, political and institutional set-ups was carried out under his enlightened leadership. His son, His Majesty Jigme Singye Wangchuck, became King in 1972 and actively pursued the policy of socio-economic and cultural progress started by his father. In present-day Bhutan there are many new roads, telecommunication facilities, hydroelectric projects, modern educational facilities; all due to the modern outlook of the present King.

In terms of average income, Bhutan is still one of the poorest countries in the world. According to estimates by the World Bank, the country's gross national product (GNP), measured at average 1979-81 prices, was only US $80 per head in both 1980 and 1981. Another estimate assessed Bhutan's GNP per head at $140 in 1984. Bhutan has some small-scale industry, producing, for example, textiles, soap, matches, candles and carpets. Centres for the production of traditional handicrafts, such as bamboo-work, lacquered woodwork and woven carpets, have been established. Several minerals of economic importance have been discovered, and small mineral-based units have been set up, such as a graphite plant at Paro.

A series of economic plans began in 1961, the first two of which were entirely financed by India. The United Nations has also provided assistance for the Fourth Plan (1976-81). Under this plan, one-half was allocated to agriculture, particularly irrigation projects. The Fifth Plan (1981-87) stressed the importance of the development of agriculture, forestry and power. Grants from the Government of India in the 1985-86 Annual Plan provided nearly 45 per cent of the total expenditure. Since 1961 considerable improvements have been achieved in roads, animal husbandry, irrigation, forestry and electricity generation. Six hydroelectric stations have been established, and exports of electricity to India were expected to begin in 1988, with the opening of the Chukha hydroelectric project. Bhutan joined the Asian Development Bank (ADB) in 1982, and received its first US $5m multi-project loan in September 1983 and a second multi-project loan of $7.4m in 1984. These loans were mainly aimed at financing agricultural equipment, the construction of roads and bridges, the development of solar power, and the improvement of water supplies and sewerage.

Since the 1960 ban on trade with Tibet, Bhutan's main trading partner has been India, although timber, alcoholic drinks and cardamom are also exported to the Middle East and Western Europe. After the inauguration of the postal system in 1962, Bhutan's postage stamps became the main source of foreign exchange, but in 1976 this category was overtaken by tourism. Economic growth was estimated at an annual average of 6 per cent in the three years to March 1982, but the rate of growth fell slightly in the year to March 1983 because of low rainfall and poor harvests.

When China invaded Tibet in 1959, Bhutan granted asylum to about 4,000 Tibetan refugees. The Government of Bhutan felt that many Tibetan refugees were engaged in spying and subversive activities, and in 1976 it was decided to disperse them in small groups, introducing a number of Bhutanese families into each settlement. Until 1978 the Tibetan refugees refused to accept Bhutanese citizenship or to leave the country. At the same time India refused to take the refugees who would not accept Bhutanese nationality. In June 1979 the National Assembly of Bhutan approved a directive which set the end of the year as a deadline for the refugees to decide whether to take out Bhutanese citizenship or accept repatriation to Tibet. By July 1980 most of the Tibetans accepted Bhutanese citizenship and the remainder were accepted by India.

Bhutan has declared itself a fully sovereign and independent state, by becoming a member of the UNO in 1971 and of the Non-Aligned Movement in 1973. It has also increased its number of diplomatic missions abroad, and in 1986 Bhutan had an Ambassador at the UN in New York, and was represented in New Delhi, Dhaka and Kathmandu. In 1983 Bhutan was an enthusiastic founder-member of the South Asian Association for Regional Cooperation (SAARC) along with Bangladesh, India, the Maldives, Nepal, Pakistan, and Sri Lanka.

The state religion is Mahayana Buddhism – *maha* means great and *yana* means salvation. It is one of the distinctive schools of

Buddhism, primarily distinguished from the older and conservative wing such as the Theravadins and the Sarvastivadins. The date of the emergence of Mahayana is difficult to determine, but it was around the first century BC to the first century AD. The Mahayana is more flexible, and more ready to incorporate new features of belief and practice, some of which were derived from popular indigenous religions; others may have reflected the strongly Graeco-Roman influence in north-western India, where Mahayana developed, such as the concept of Divine Wisdom or Transcendental Wisdom. The teaching of Mahayana is more distinctly religious, making its appeal to the heart and not the mind, to the intuition rather than the intellect. It seeks the spiritual interpretation of the verbal teaching and endeavours to expound that teaching in a variety of forms calculated to appeal to every type of mind and every stage of spiritual development. For this reason it calls itself the Great or Universal Vehicle. Yet it fully recognizes that this method is only a concession to man's limitations, an accommodation of Truth to the intelligence of the hearer. Mahayana discountenances asceticism of any kind, its Sangha (the monastic order founded by the Buddha) being a body of teachers rather than monks. It is pantheistic rather than atheistic. The goal of Mahayana is Bodhisattva (the wisdom resulting from direct perception of Truth) and renunciation of Nirvana (release from the limitations of existence) in order to help humanity in its pilgrimage towards that goal.

According to the Bhutanese tradition, an Indian saint named Padma Sambhava or Pema Jungney (one who was born from a lotus flower), more popularly known as Guru Rimpoche (precious teacher), arrived in Bhutan around 800 AD. He is the founder of the Nyingmapa (an old school of Himalayan Buddhism), and introduced in Tibet and Bhutan tantric Buddhism (a highly esoteric form of the Mahayana Buddhism). In the thirteenth century Phajo Drugom Shigpo made the Drukpa school of Kagyupa Buddhism dominant in Bhutan, and this sect is still supported by the dominant race in Bhutan, the Drukpas. At present the main monastic group (comprising 1,160 monks), is led by an elected Head Abbot (Je Khempo) and is directly supported by the state, while a further 2,120 monks are sustained by the lay population. The Central Board for Monastic Affairs, established in 1984, oversees all religious bodies. Monasteries (Gompas) and shrines (Lhakhangs) are numerous. The chief monastery is situated at Tashichhodzong and contains about 2,000 lamas (Buddhist priests). There are about 5,000 state-supported lamas in the kingdom, with the Je Khempo as their elected head. In southern Bhutan, the Nepali population of Bhutan are Hindus.

Introduction

About the bibliography

Bhutan is one of those countries on which only a limited amount of material has been written in English, but this bibliography should enable a student, or researcher, to gain a comprehensive knowledge of the area. The state is distinct in its history, politics, languages, economic development and modernization programmes, and all these are worthy of careful study. This volume reflects the nature of the work published in English from the British period to the present day. The work began with a check-list based on books and periodicals in the School of Oriental and African Studies Library, University of London. Next, material in other UK libraries was surveyed and a similar check-list prepared. In the end, about 85 per cent of the material on the check-list was examined and annotated; the rest of the material was either missing, not available, or not worth including in the bibliography. Entries in each section are arranged alphabetically by the author's surname.

Acknowledgements

First of all I would like to thank the many authors and institutions from all over the world who have taken an interest in Bhutan and published books and articles on the country. Without their work the task of this compiler would have been impossible, and our knowledge of Bhutan impaired. Thanks are also due to Clio Press for including the project as part of their noted 'World Bibliographical Series', and my particular thanks go to Dr Robert G. Neville (Executive Editor) for help and criticism extended to me during the completion of this volume. I am also grateful to Rahul Dogra for checking the manuscript and making some useful suggestions, and Ambika Dogra in helping me in arranging the index and drawing the map of Bhutan. My thanks are also due to my wife who at different times rendered most valuable bibliographical assistance. Her willingness to spend time in chasing items for me, in addition to pursuing her own work, is gratefully acknowledged.

Ramesh C. Dogra
September 1990

Chronology

500 BC-500 AD	Prehistoric Mon Yul – South Sandalwood country. Bonism, the prevalent religion.
500 AD	Bon leader Lhasa Tsangpa comes to Tashigang.
640	King Srongtesen Gampo establishes Buddhist monasteries – Kheychu monastery at Paro, and Jampa Lhakhang at Bumthang.
747	Guru Rimpoche or Limpoche (original name Padma Sambhava) visits Bhutan. Guru Rimpoche came from northern India to spread Buddhism in Bhutan, and founded Nyingmapa school of Buddhism.
816-836	Incursion of Mongoloid troops into Bhutan during the rule of Tibetan King Ralpachen.
830	Lam Tsangpa arrives in Bhutan to spread Buddhism.
836-842	Lang Darma drives Buddhism out of Tibet.
1153	Gyalwa Lhanangpa of Nyo-sect comes to Bhutan from Deloung.
1200	Phajo Drugom Shigpo establishes his authority in Bhutan, and spreads the Drukpa school of Buddhism.
1251	Death of Phajo Drugom Shigpo.
1350	The great Nyingmapa philosopher Longchen Rabjampa (1308-63) comes to Bhutan.
1361	Lam Ne Nyingmpa comes to Bhutan.
1450	Lam Drukpa Kunlay comes to Bhutan.
1616	Ngawang Namgyal, a scion of the house of Gya of Druk and Ralung and the head of the Druk school of the Kagyupa, arrives in Bhutan. He proclaims Bhutan a theocracy and becomes spiritual head and ruler of Bhutan.
1620	Shabdrung Ngawang Namgyal establishes Chari monastery.
1627	Jesuit missionaries Estevão Cacella and João Cabral of Goa and Portugal visit Bhutan and Tibet.
1629	Shabdung Ngawang Namgyal constructs a new Dzong on the site of the old Dongon Dzong and names it Tashichho Dzong.

Chronology

1806	Umze Parop becomes Deb.
1807	Boep Choeda becomes Deb.
1809	Shabdrung Jigme Dragpa becomes Deb.
1811	Chhogley Yeshe Gyaltshen becomes Deb.
1815	Tshaphu Dorji becomes Deb.
1819	Tenzin Drugda ascends the Golden Throne.
1823	Choeki Gyaltshen ascends the Golden Throne.
1832	Dorji Namgyal ascends the Golden Throne.
1833	Adap Thrinley becomes Deb.
1835	Choeki Gyaltshen becomes Deb.
1837	Pemberton's mission to Bhutan.
1838	Dorji Norbu ascends the Golden Throne.
1841	The British annex the Bhutan Duars on the Assam border.
1850	Wangchhug Gyalpo ascends the Golden Throne.
1851	Shabdrung Tuelku Jigme Norbu ascends the Golden Throne, and Chagpa Sangye becomes Deb.
1852	Lopon Bachup Damchhoe Lhundup becomes Deb.
1856	Kuenga Palden Sonam Tobgyel becomes Deb.
1860	Nagzi Pasang Phuntsho Namgyal becomes Deb.
1863	Tshewang Sithub becomes Deb.
1864	Kaju Wangchhug ascends the Golden Throne. Ashley Eden's mission to Bhutan. Anglo-Bhutanese war.
1865	Treaty of peace between Bhutan and India. Tsulthrim Yonten becomes Deb. Tshenyi Lopen Tseundue becomes Deb.
1870	Jigme Namgyal ascends the Golden Throne.
1874	Kitshap Dorji Namgyal ascends the Golden Throne.
1877	Civil war in Bhutan.
1879	Chhoegyal Zangpo ascends the Golden Throne.
1882	Lam Tshewang becomes Deb.
1884	Gawa Zangpo becomes Deb.
1885	Civil war in Bhutan.
1886	Pam Sangye Dorji becomes Deb.
1897	Punakha Dzong destroyed by earthquake.
1903	Chhoegyal Teelku Yeshey Ngoedub becomes Deb.
1906	Birth of Gyalse Jigme Wangchuck.
1907	Ugyen Wangchuck elected as the hereditary king of Bhutan.
1910	Anglo-Bhutanese treaty signed.
1911	Ugyen Wangchuck attends the Delhi Darbar.
1912	Lord Ronaldshay visits Bhutan.
1926	Death of Drug Gyalpo Ugyen Wangchuck.
1927	Gyalse Jigme Wangchuck ascends the Golden Throne of Bhutan.
1928	Birth of Gyalse Jigme Dorji Wangchuck.

Chronology

1947	Bhutan attends Asian Relations Conference in Delhi.
1949	Indo-Bhutanese treaty signed.
1952	King Jigme Wangchuck passes away.
	King Jigme Dorji Wangchuck ascends the Golden Throne.
1953	Establishment of the Tshogdu – National Assembly of Bhutan.
1954	King Jigme Dorji Wangchuck visits India.
1955	Birth of Gyalse Jigme Singye.
1958	Prime Minister Jawaharlal Nehru visits Bhutan.
1961	Bhutan inaugurates the First Five-Year Development Plan.
1962	Bhutan attends as Observer the Colombo Plan Meeting at Melbourne.
	Modern postal system was introduced.
1963	Bhutan joins the Colombo Plan.
1965	Establishment of the Royal Advisory Council.
1966	Bhutan's Second Five-Year Plan started.
1968	King Jigme Dorji Wangchuck becomes a constitutional monarch.
1969	Bhutan becomes a member of International Postal Union.
1970	Bhutan attends the UN General Assembly as Observer.
1971	Bhutan becomes a Member of the United Nations.
	Third Five-Year Plan started.
1972	Planning Commission of Bhutan constituted.
	King Jigme Dorji Wangchuck passes away.
	Prince Jigme Singye Wangchuck becomes King.
1974	Coronation of King Jigme Singye Wangchuck.
	Bhutan opened to tourism in 1974.
1976	Fourth Five-Year Plan started.
1981	Fifth Five-Year Plan started.
1982	Bhutan becomes a member of UNESCO.
1986	Asian Development Bank approved a loan of $4.5m towards roadworks mechanization project in Bhutan.
1987	Sixth Five-Year Plan started.

Chronology of Rulers and Dignitaries of Bhutan

Druk Shabdung Lama 1616-1907

1594-1651	Ngawang Namgyal
1724-61	Ngawang Jigme Dakpa
1762-88	Ngawang Chhokyi Gyaltsen
1791-1830	Ngawang Jigme Dakpa
1831-61	Ngawang Jigme Norbu
1862-1903	Ngawang Jigme Chhogyal

Druk Deb 1651-1905

1651-56	Umze Tenzin Druggyal
1657-68	Langonpa Tenzin Drugda
1668-76	Chhogyal Mingyur Tempa
1680-94	Tenzin Rabgye
1694-1702	Karbi Gedun Chhophel
1702-4	Ngawang Tsering
1704-8	Penjor
1708-20	Drug Rabgye
1720-29	Geshe Ngawang Gyatso
1729-37	Rimpochhe Mipham Wangpo
1738-39	Kuo Penjor
1740-44	Sachong Ngawang Gyaltsen
1744-63	Chhogyal Sherab Wangchuk
1763-65	Druk Phuntsok
1765-68	Druk Tenzin
1768-73	Sonam Lhendup
1773-75	Tsanlob Kunga Rinchhen
1776-89	Jigme Senge
1789-91	Druk Tenzin
1792-98	Sonam Gyaltsen
1798-99	Umze Chapchapa
1799-1803	Druk Namgyal
1803	Umze Sonam Gyaltsen

Chronology of Rulers and Dignitaries of Bhutan

1803-6	Sangye Tenzin
1806-8	Umzepa Dowa and Bopa Choda
1808	Shabdung Jigme Dakpa
1809	Tsulthim Dakpa
1810	Shabdung Jigme Dakpa
1811-15	Chhole Tulku Yeshe Gyaltsen
1815	Tsaphu Dorje
1815-19	Miwang Sonam Druggyal
1819-23	Tenzin Drukda
1823-31	Chhokyi Gyatso
1831-33	Dorji Namgyal
1833-35	Atangpa Thinle
1835-38	Chhokyi Gyatso
1838-49	Dorje Norbu
1849-50	Tashi Dorje
1850	Wangchuk Gyalpo
1850	Shabdung Jigme Norbu
1850-52	Chakpa Sangye
1857-58	Dorlob Parchung
1858-60	Sonam Tobgye
1860-63	Phuntsok Namgyal
1863	Tsulthim Yonten
1864	Kagyu Wangchuck
1864-65	Tsewang Situp
1865	Tsondu Pekar
1870-74	Jigme Namgyal
1874-78	Kyitselpa Dorje Namgyal
1878-81	Chhogyal Zangpo
1881-82	Lama Tsewang
1882-83	Kawa Zangpo
1883-1901	Yanglob Sangye Dorje
1901-5	Chhole Tulku Yeshe Ngodub

Druk Gyalpo 1907 (title of the King of Bhutan)

1907-26	Ugyen Wangchuck
1926-52	Jigme Wangchuck
1952-72	Jigme Dorji Wangchuck
1972-	Jigme Singye Wangchuck

Glossary

Amban	Chinese representative stationed in Lhasa in Tibet
Arhat	A saint who has overcome greed, hatred and delusion
Arupa	Formless, incorporeal. The heavenly world where form cognizable by the five senses does not exist, being purely mental
Asavas	Mental intoxication, defilement. The four *Asavas* are: *kama* (sensuality), *bhava* (lust), *dittha* (delusion), and *avijja* (ignorance)
Ashi	Princess
Asuras	Demons or anti-gods
Asvaghosa	Buddhist scholar, philosopher, poet, and musician, born of brahmin parents in Ayodhya, India (?80 BC–AD 150?)
Attavada	The doctrine of belief in a persistent soul or self
Bardo	Intermediate state between death and rebirth
Belo	Hat made of bamboo
Bhavana	Self-development by any means, but especially by the method of mind control, concentration and meditation
Bhikkhu or Bhikshu	A Buddhist monk, mendicant. A Bhikhu is one who has devoted himself to the task of following the path by renunciation of the distractions of worldly affairs
Boku or *kho*	Bhutanese male dress
Bon	The indigenous, pre-Buddhist, religion of Tibet

Glossary

Chamai Chichap	Master of dance
Chenzi	Thin strip of silk or brocade hung in symmetrical undulating patterns
Chhang	Local beer
Chhoje	Literally it means Lord Spiritual, a form of address for any descendant of Shabdung Ngawang Namgyal or for a scion of any of the ancient religious families of Bhutan
Chhosi	Dual system of administration where both the clergy and laity were associated in governing the country
Chhura	Yellow bear
Chila	Short for Chichap Lama, title of a regional governor in Bhutan
Chorten (stupa)	A building where sacred relics are enshrined
Chu	Stream, river or water
Churpi	Dried cheese
Dapon	Officer of high military rank next to Magpon (General). The word Dapon literally means 'arrow chief' and refers to an officer of the rank of a Colonel in the army
Dasho	Term of address and title given to anyone in high office in Bhutan
Deb	Like Depa or Desi of Tibet, Deb was the title of the head of the temporal side of the Government of Bhutan up to the establishment of the monarchy in 1907
Deb Raja	The same as Deb
Deva Loka	The abode of gods
Dharma	Virtue, religion, duty, law; and in the context of Buddhism the law propagated by Lord Buddha
Dharmas	Nine Mahayana scriptures considered of supreme importance as containing complete exposition of exoteric and esoteric teachings of Buddha. They are called Vaipula Sutras, and they comprise: Ashtasahasrika Prajnaparamita; Ganda-vyuha; Dasabhumisvara; Samadhi-raja; Lankavatara Sutra; Sad-

	dharma-Pundarika; Tathagatha-guhyaka; Lalita-vistara; and Suvarna-prabhasa
Dhyana	Mystic states of serene contemplation attained by meditation
Dorje	Thunderbolt sceptre
Dremo	Blue bear
Druk	Dragon
Drukdom	Compulsory work according to which a family consisting of six male members between the ages of eighteen and fifty deputed one person for government work for a specified period on payment of wages
Druk Gyalpo	Title of the King of Bhutan
Drukpa	Follower of the Drukpa sect of Buddhism; broadly speaking a native of Bhutan
Drukpa Kagyu	The state religion of Bhutan
Dudjom	One who can conquer evil spirits
Dukha	Suffering
Dzong	Castle, fortress. Also the headquarters of a district where the Dzongpon and his staff live. Fortified castle and monastery in Bhutan. Seat of religious and administrative hierarchy of a particular area
Dzongda	District administrator. Chief of a District
Dzongpon	Chief official in charge of a fortress and district. The term Dzongpon disappeared from Bhutan's administrative parlance with the acceptance of the term Thimpon in 1954
Dzongtsab	Deputy Dzongpon
Gap	Village headman
Gelong	A fully ordained monk
Geshe	A high scholarly degree in the Lama hierarchy, like the degree of the Doctor of Divinity in the Christian hierarchy
Gonkhang	Temple devoted to guardian deities
Gup	A Bhutanese village headman. Gup is the Bhutanese version of Gopa, a village headman in Tibet

Glossary

Guru	Teacher or preceptor
Gya Chila	Short for Gyagar Chichap Lama. Title of the Bhutanese agent in Cooch Bihar (India) in 1765-73
Gyaldon	Chief Secretary, next to King
Gyalwa Karmapa	Head of the Kagyupa sect of Buddhism
Gyase	Crown prince (literally, son)
Gyuying	Running script
Jampa	The Buddha of the future
Je Khempo	Lord Abbot. Head of the monastic establishment of the Government of Bhutan, usually elected for three years. The word is generally used in its short form Je Khem. The hierarchical practice is to address the Je Khempo as Je Khempo Rimpichhe.
Kagyup	Semi-reformed sect of the Buddhism of Tibet founded by Marpa (1012-97) and his disciples
Kasho	Royal command
Kera	A belt used by both men and women
Khang	House
Kira	Woman's dress
Khyilkhor (mandala)	A mystic circle
Lama	Spiritual teacher and guide. The expression Lama corresponds to the Sanskrit expression – Guru. In Bhutan the word is generally abbreviated to Lam especially when it is prefixed as a title to the name of a Lama
Lhakhang	Temple
Lhengye	That section of society which had the rank of Minister and above
Lhengye Tsok	State Council
Lho Mon	Short for Lho Mon Kha Shi, four southern lowlands in Bhutan. Traditional name for Bhutan
Lhotsam Chichap	Southern Commissioner
Lobpon	Teacher

Lochak	Embassy from one country to another for the presentation of customary gifts. Druk Lochak carried gifts from Bhutan to Tibet annually
Lodro Tshogde	Royal Advisory Council
Lonpo or Lyonpo	Minister or Counsellor
Losar	New Year
Mahakali	A Hindu goddess
Mahaparinirvana	Great, final Nirvana, outwardly coinciding with death
Mahasiddhas	Persons who attain enlightenment while performing their worldly duties
Mandala	A sacred circle formed by gems, grains, powder, etc. and used as a ceremonial offering to deities
Mantra	Symbolic evocative sound or word of spiritual power
Manusya Loka	Realm of man
Marmedze	The Buddha of the past
Mathra	A type of woollen cloth produced locally
Maya	Illusion
Narka Loka	Hell
Nirvana	Enlightenment
Nutam	Silver coin
Om Mane Padma Haun (Hymn)	A prayer used by the Mongol, Tartar and Tibetan Buddhists. It is commonly translated by the words, 'Oh! the jewel in the lotus', but the literal translation is (Om – God), (Mane – jewel), (Padma – lotus), (Haun – that is so). This invocation is quite unknown to the Buddhist of Ceylon or the Eastern Peninsula, and forms the peculiar feature of Tibetan Buddhism
Padma Sambhava	The 'Lotus Born', a native of northern India who spread Buddhism in Bhutan and Tibet
Palang	Wine casket
Pangchu	Basket made of cane or bamboo
Parikrama	Circumambulation

Glossary

Pasu Loka	Realm of animals
Pawo	A local oracle
Penlop	Governor
Phurba	A triple-bladed dagger used in Tantric rituals
Ponkha Tsok	Council of Ministers (literally, Council of Chief Officials)
Ponlop	Title of a regional Governor in Bhutan
Preta Loka	Realm of unsatisfied spirits
Ramjam	A junior official. Title of a junior civil servant in Bhutan
Rimpoche	Precious jewel. This honorific title is usually given to a great and learned teacher. A Rimpoche is usually a reincarnate, but also one who attains this stage by his own efforts
Sakyapa	Semi-reformed sect of the Buddhism of Tibet. Sakya is a place in Central Tibet. The main monastery of the Sakyapa is there
Samsara	Temporal world
Shacha Thupa	The Buddha of the present age (Sakya Muni)
Shugdrel	A religious ceremony performed
Siddhi	Spiritual or mystic power
Sunkho	A portable temple which people carry while travelling
Sunyata	Metaphysical emptiness; 'plenum void'
Ta dzong	A watch tower; citadel overlooking the main dzong
Tanga	Coin. This is a word from modern Tibetan
Tanka	*See* Thangka
Tashi koma	A mobile temple containing many doors
Tashi Tagye	The eight auspicious signs
Tatshang	Monastic colleges maintained by the state
Terma	Spiritual treasure
Terton	One who discovers hidden spiritual treasure
Thangka	A religious painting or scroll
Thimpon	Means 'law chief', and refers to an officer of the rank and position of a magistrate in the civil administration

Thondrol	A religious painting or scroll (*thangka*) of a very big size
Thrimpon	Judicial head of a district
Tikchung	Bhutanese coin equivalent to half an Indian rupee
Timmi	Lime container
Torma	A sacrificial cake
Tsabda	Brigadier
Tsa yik	Ordinances
Tsampa	Barley flour
Tsechu	Annual festival held in all valleys to propitiate the local deities
Tshogdu	National Assembly
Tsongdu	The same as Tshogdu
Tsongkhapa	A great Tibetan reformer (1355-1417)
Tsepame (Amitayu)	Buddha of long life
Umze	Head Lama of a dzong (monastery)
Yama	Lord of death
Yogi	An ascetic
Zimpon	Chief of household. Also called Gongzim.

The Country and Its People

1 **Nepal, Sikkim und Bhutan: Reiseführer mit Stadtführer Kathmandu, Wander- und Bergtouren.** (Nepal, Sikkim and Bhutan: a guidebook; including a town guide to Kathmandu, walking tours and mountain tours.)
Jan Boon.   Munich, West Germany: Verlag 'Volk und Heimat', 1976. 5th ed. 137p. maps.

The first part of the book considers Nepal and provides detailed information. The second and third parts cover Sikkim and Bhutan and are fairly brief. Pages 122 to 136 relate to Bhutan and provide useful information about its people, places of interest, history, geography, religion, agriculture, handicrafts and export items. This guide provides useful hints about the Himalayan states.

2 **South Asia: the changing environment.**
Edited by Charanjit Chanana.   New Delhi: Merb Bookshelf, 1979. 266p.

The book contains eighteen chapters relating to economic cooperation in South Asia together with a consideration of US and Chinese policies in the Indian subcontinent. Pages 6-7, 60-2, and 160-1 contain figures of the annual birth and death rates in Bhutan and its estimated population in 1975 along with a projected figure for the year 2000. Some information on rural and urban population as a percentage of total population of Bhutan is provided for the years 1980, 1990 and 2000. There is also a comparison of the strength of the armed forces of Bhutan and South Asia with America, USSR and China.

3 **Sikkim and Bhutan.**
V. H. Coelho.   Delhi: Indian Council for Cultural Relations, Vikas Publications, 1971. 138p.

This work is intended for tourists and those who wish to gain a greater appreciation of the unknown and beautiful places hidden away in the Himalayas. It contains a useful vocabulary of Bhutanese words and their English equivalents, and the places of

1

The Country and Its People

religious and historical interest are also included. Information is also provided about the land, the people, their customs and their system of government.

4 **Bhutan: Kultur und Religion im Land der Drachenkönige.** (Bhutan: Culture and religion in the land of the dragon kings.)
Manfred Gerner.   Stuttgart, West Germany: Verlag Indoculture, 1981. 194p. maps. bibliog.

This survey is intended for the general reader. It includes information on the history of the country from the seventh to the nineteenth century, together with brief biographical sketches of the kings of Bhutan from 1900 onwards, monasteries and holy places of great interest in central and eastern Bhutan, and the mask dances of Bhutan. The information is well supported with illustrations.

5 **Area handbook for Nepal, Bhutan and Sikkim.**
George L. Harris, Jackson A. Giddens, Thomas E. Lux, Frederica M. Bunge, Frances Chadwick Rintz, Harvey H. Smith.   Washington, DC: American University, Foreign Area Studies, 1973. 2nd ed. 431p. map. bibliog.

This very useful handbook prepared by Foreign Area Studies is designed to be useful to military and other personnel who need a convenient compilation of basic facts about the social, economic, political and military institutions and practices of various countries. On Bhutan (pages 345-77) it includes information on the size of the country and its population, boundaries, strategic passes, mountains, rivers, flora and fauna, climate, history, politics, political dynamics, key political figures, defence matters, religion, the society, land use, land tenure, agriculture and animal husbandry, forestry, minerals, power, industry, handicrafts, trade, transport and social development.

6 **Report from Bhutan.**
E. Burke Inlow.   *Asian Affairs*, vol. 9, no. 3 (Oct. 1978), p. 295-308.

Dr Inlow, Professor of Political Science at the University of Calgary, Alberta, provides a general history of Bhutan and examines the essential characteristics of the people of the country. He thinks that the people are still the same and do not appear to have changed very much since George Bogle wrote about them in 1774. Bogle noted that the people were 'simple, good mannered, honest, good humoured, thoroughly trustworthy, sturdy and hardworking'. The author also describes briefly the ethnic and tribal distinctions, politics of the country from 1910 to 1972, and the economic progress of Bhutan due to the Five-Year Plans which started in 1961. Some discussion about radical changes which were initiated in the social and economic sphere of the country, and political and religious reforms introduced in 1972, are also included.

7 **Tiny kingdom high in the sky.**
Pradyumna P. Karan.   In: *The nations of Asia*, edited by Donald Newton Wilber, maps by Delos D. Rowe Associates. New York: Hart, 1966, p. 64-77.

The author, an oustanding authority on Bhutan, provides a good picture of: Bhutan's inner and outer Himalayas; religion; education; rural population; economy; history; government; trade; and transport and communications. The text is supported by black-and-white illustrations and a map of the country.

2

8   **The Himalaya: aspects of change.**
Edited by J. S. Lall, in association with A. D. Moddie.   Delhi: Oxford
University Press, 1981. 481p. bibliog.

This is a general book on the Himalayan region. The first section deals with its climate,
geology, soils, flora, fauna and water resources. Bhutan is featured on pages 30, 36-7
and 65-9. The second section deals with the Himalayan communities and their response
to changes and new developments in the outside world. The studies in this section
reveal in some measure the extraordinary complexity of change in Himalayan
communities. Bhutan is examined on pages 240-4 and 296-303, and these also include
information on Pandit Nehru's visit to Bhutan in 1958 and on an agreement struck with
the King of Bhutan that the construction of roads to link the interior provinces of
Bhutan with the plains of India was to be achieved with technical personnel,
equipment and finance to be provided by the Government of India.

9   **Les royaumes de l'Himalaya: histoire et civilisation. Le Ladakh, le
Bhoutan, le Sikkim, le Népal.** (The kingdoms of the Himalaya: history and
civilisation. Ladakh, Bhutan, Sikkim, Nepal.)
A. W. Macdonald, Ch. Massonaud, Ph. Sagant, A. Vergati.   Paris:
Imprimerie nationale, 1982. 249p. 6 maps. bibliog.

The authors draw our attention to the Buddhist expansion of the Mahayana system in
these Himalayan kingdoms. The third chapter of the book is on Bhutan and deals with
its geography, trade, history, society, religion and the arts. It is a vivid chapter, full of
information. There are a number of plates throughout the book which contain good
photographs taken by the authors.

10   **Le Bhoutan.** (Bhutan.)
Chantal Massonaud. In: *Les royaumes de l'Himalaya: histoire et
civilisation. Le Ladakh, le Bhoutan, le Sikkim, le Népal*, by A. W.
MacDonald (et al.), p. 67-116.   Paris: Imprimerie nationale, 1982.
maps.

This chapter of a more general book (q.v.) covers geography, history and society
(composition of the people, languages, costumes); the religion of the people and
monasteries; and also architecture, sculpture and literature.

11   **Bhutan: land of the peaceful dragon.**
G. N. Mehra.   Delhi: Vikas, 1974. 151p.

In 1971 Bhutan became a member of the United Nations, and in the same year Mehra
was requested by the King of Bhutan (Druk Gyalpo Jigme Dorje Wangchuck, 1952-72)
to write a book on Bhutan which would give an accurate and comprehensive picture of
the country which was striving towards modernization, while at the same time seeking
to retain all the good things about its ancient culture and religion. It is designed to
provide information on Bhutan's social life, art, architecture, religion, philosophy,
early history, and the system of administration in the country together with its efforts
towards modernization. The text of the book is well supported by the photographs
taken by the author.

The Country and Its People

12 **Bhutan: an introductory note.**
Chandra Das Rai. *United Asia*, vol. 12, no. 4 (1960), p. 365-8.
In this general article on the people, culture, economy, history and administration of the country, Rai also provides a general survey of the political system from 1907 to 1960, together with Bhutan's achievements in trade and industry, education, and health care.

13 **Lost world: Tibet, key to Asia.**
Amaury De Riencourt. London: Gollancz, 1951. 317p.
This volume provides information on the history, government, politics and social life in Tibet, together with the rule of the thirteenth Dalai Lama and Tibet in the twentieth century. With reference to Bhutan (pages 20-2, 36-7, 166-7 and various others, passim) the author points out that all the princely and aristocratic families of various Himalayan states are related to each other. These interrelationships are seen, for example, in the effect of the 1908 political disturbances in Tibet on the royal family of Bhutan as their son-in-law was in jail in Lhasa (Tibet) for his involvement in a plot against the regent of Tibet. It is also explained why the Dalai Lama in 1910 decided to go to India instead of seeking refuge in Bhutan which was only two miles away.

14 **Bhutan today.**
N. K. Rustomji. *Bulletin of Tibetology*, vol. 3, no. 1 (Feb. 1966), p. 64-70.
As a result of the author's travels throughout the country, the article provides a general view of Bhutan in the mid-1960s. There is a clear picture of the extent of economic aid received from India and of the slow economic progress in the country. The author highlights what, on the strength of his own experience, he regards as the main changes which have occurred in Bhutan between 1950 and 1965.

15 **Bhutan: a kingdom in the Himalayas. A study of the land, its people and their government.**
Nagendra Singh. New Delhi: Thomson Press (India), 1972. 202p. map. bibliog.
At the time this book was published, the author was a constitutional adviser to the government of Bhutan and Judge Ad Hoc of the International Court of Justice. It is a study of the history, culture and politics of the sovereign state of Bhutan. The book is divided into three parts: Part 1 deals with land, people, history, art, culture and religion; Part 2 deals with the state and its government, political institutions, the organizations of government and economic development in Bhutan; and Part 3 describes Bhutan's entry to the United Nations Organization (UNO) and its welcome into the World Family of Nations by various countries of the world. The appendixes include the principal animals and birds of Bhutan, articles of the Treaty of Peace between the Honourable East India Company and the Deb Raja of Bhutan in 1774, the treaty between India and Bhutan in 1949, etc. A number of coloured photographs are included, depicting the life of the people.

16 **A short account of the eastern Himalayan states of Sikkim, Bhutan and Tibet.**
    J. Claude White. *Journal of the East India Association (new series)*, vol. 4 (1913), p. 170-80.

This is a useful article introducing Bhutan, Tibet and Sikkim together with their countryside, people, religion, and physical features.

17 **Asia: a handbook.**
    Edited by Guy Wint. New York: Praeger, 1966; London: Blond, 1967. 856p.

The handbook contains 81 essays by 60 contributors of international standing and predominantly British. It provides (on pages 83-5) information about Bhutan's history and about the Indo-China border dispute on the northern frontiers of Bhutan. The book has an analytical index.

Geography and Geology

General

18 **Water resources policy for Asia.**
Edited by Mohammed Ali. Rotterdam: A. A. Balkema, 1987. 627p.
Intended for the general reader as well as the specialist, this collection of papers was
the result of a 'Regional symposium on water resources policy in agro-socio-economic
development' held in Dhaka from 4 to 8 August 1985. Topics covered include water
resources, water management, utilization and consumption of water, and case-studies
of Bangladesh, Bhutan, Indonesia, Malaysia, the Maldives, Pakistan, the Philippines,
and Thailand.

19 **Human ecology in Bhutan and modernizing trends.**
Anima Bhattacharyya. In: *The Himalayas: profiles of modernisation
and adaptation*, edited by S. K. Chaube. New Delhi: Sterling, 1985,
p. 17-25. bibliog.
This chapter (the third in the volume) provides a geographical view of Bhutanese
society, the physical environment, vegetation, economy, geographical background, and
settlement patterns. It also surveys development trends in the fields of agriculture,
industry and house-building, and some of the ill effects of modern development.

20 **Patterns of relationship between land and resources and population in
Bhutan.**
W. A. Bladen. *Asian Profile*, vol. 11, no. 4 (Aug. 1983), p. 411-18.
The author, an Associate Professor of Geography at the University of Kentucky,
provides a map of the land support units in each district of Bhutan and assesses how
much land is required to produce food in order to support the population in that area.
The situation of the cultivated land and the availability of water for cultivation are
analysed in order to find out how the productivity of the land can be raised, so as to be
self-sufficient. The author believes that the map provided in this article, which shows

land use along with the distribution of population, and his interpretation in terms of historical, economic, and demographic responses to development, should provide the factual basis needed for planning decisions. He also provides a map of cultivated land, forest and mountain pasture, glaciers, and some isolated grazing and farming areas in the mountain valleys.

21 **Notes on the valley of Choombi.**
Archibald Campbell. *Journal of the Royal Asiatic Society of Great Britain and Ireland*, vol. 7 (1874), p. 135-9.

Chumbi Valley is a slip of territory belonging mostly to Tibet and partly to Bhutan and Sikkim. It lies between the north-western boundary of Bhutan and the eastern boundary of Sikkim, and covers about 53 miles in the north-eastern district of Darjeeling (West Bengal). The author, formerly Superintendent of Darjeeling, describes the physical features of the valley as well as events in the region which involved Bhutan, Sikkim and Tibet.

22 **Geology of the Himalayas.**
Augusto Gansser. London; New York; Sydney: Interscience, 1964. 289p. maps. bibliog. (Regional Geology Series).

Augusto Gansser, Professor of Geology in the University of Zurich, Switzerland, provides a geological account of the entire Himalayan region. Chapter eight (p. 173-218) deals with Sikkim (India), Bhutan and the Himalayas. This part of the Himalayan range measures about 400 kilometres and includes the lower and higher Himalayas of Bhutan. The final section of the book deals with the geological history of the region as a whole.

23 **Bhutan and the Himalayas east of Darjeeling.**
Henry H. Godwin-Austen. *Scottish Geographical Magazine*, vol. 10 (1894), p. 635-40.

The author read a paper with this title before the British Association at Oxford in 1894, giving an account of his experience while accompanying the mission of the late Sir Ashley Eden to Punakha (Bhutan) in 1863-64. He provides information about the geographical features of the country, and an excellent description of the difficulties of reaching Bhutan. The article is a most readable account of the country, mountains, forests, and the weather.

24 **Stratigraphy and tectonic﹐ of parts of eastern Bhutan.**
B. S. Jangpangi. In: *Himalayan geology*, edited by A. G. Jhingran. New Delhi: Wadia Institute of Himalayan Geology, 1971-75, vol. 4, p. 117-36.

Scientists had little knowledge of the geology of eastern Bhutan until the 1960s. This article is based on information gained from fieldwork carried out by the author between 1963 and 1966 in eastern Bhutan. It places particular emphasis on the stratigraphy and tectonics of Thimpu, Shumar and the Gong Ri valley areas.

25 **Sikkim and Bhutan.**

B. K. Kapur. *Commonwealth Journal*, vol. 5 (Nov.-Dec. 1962), p. 275-7.

The text of a speech given at the Ceylon Branch of the Royal Commonwealth Society in 1962. The speech includes a good description of these two Himalayan kingdoms together with an analysis of the strategic role which they then played in world affairs.

26 **Bhutan: a physical and cultural geography.**

Pradyumna P. Karan. Lexington, Kentucky: University of Kentucky Press, 1967. 103p. map. bibliog.

Recent events had focused interests on the study of the history, politics, and the strategic position of Bhutan. Subjects such as its land, people, and economy had not been studied and therefore required intensive research. Karan claims that his is the first geographical survey of either Bhutan's physical or cultural landscape. The study includes geographical exploration, contemporary politics, physiographical setting, climatic conditions, vegetation, soil, economic pattern, population and settlement pattern, cultural pattern, transport, trade and economic development.

27 **The Himalayan kingdoms: Bhutan, Sikkim, and Nepal.**

Pradyumna P. Karan, William M. Jenkins. Princeton, New Jersey: Van Nostrand, 1963. 144p.

This book represents an attempt to evaluate the complex politico-geographical pattern of the Himalayan kingdoms. On pages 27-55 it offers a short and concise history of Bhutan in addition to an assessment of its geographical situation, economics, transport development, changes in Bhutan, boundaries with India and China, government and world relations. Fieldwork in Sikkim and Bhutan during the years 1961-62 provided the material for this useful and informative essay.

28 **Ground water in continental Asia (Central, Eastern, Southern South-Eastern Asia).**

UN Department of Technical Co-operation for Development. New York: United Nations, 1986. 391p. (Natural resources/water series, no. 15).

The subjects covered in this book include groundwater, hydrology, geology, and the climate of such countries as Bhutan, Afghanistan, Democratic Kampuchea, India, Lao PDR, Malaysia, the Maldives, Mongolia, Nepal, Pakistan, Korea and Singapore.

29 **Oil and natural gas resources in the ESCAP region: geology, reserves, production, potential, distribution.**

UN ESCAP. Natural Resources Division, Mineral Resources Section. Bangkok: ESCAP, 1987. 154p. (Mineral concentrations and hydrocarbon accumulations in the ESCAP region, vol. 2).

This book provides information on consumption, production, foreign trade, offshore exploration, sedimentary basins, hydrocarbon resources, petroleum exploration, petroleum reserves, natural gas reserves, oil fields and gas fields. It covers Afghanistan, Australia, Bangladesh, Bhutan, Brunei, Darusalam and Burma.

Maps, atlases and gazetteers

30   Atlas of the northern frontier of India.
New Delhi: Ministry of External Affairs, 1960. 39 folded maps.
This dated, but still interesting, atlas contains a representative collection of maps which support the official Indian view that the northern frontier of India, as shown on official Indian maps, is the traditional boundary between India and China. These official and non-official Indian, Chinese, British, French and German maps have been showing this boundary alignment for many years. Most of the maps contain Bhutan and its boundaries. About five maps also show the McMahon Line – the Indo-Chinese border line, drawn in March 1914 at a British-Tibetan-Chinese conference in Simla and named after a British administrator. Communist China, which has absorbed Tibet, repudiated the McMahon Line as delimiting her border with India, but India insists that it is a legitimate and a legal border-line.

31   The gazetteer of Sikkim.
Edited in the Bengal Government Secretariat, with an introduction by
H. H. Risley.   New Delhi: Mansuri, 1972. 392p.
A general introduction to Sikkim is followed by detailed articles by various authors (H. H. Risley, J. C. White, P. N. Bose, J. A. Gammie, L. de Niceville, L. A. Waddell) on the geography, geology, mineral resources, agriculture, vegetation, butterflies, reptiles, birds, mammals, law and religion (Buddhist temples, description of village priest, monasteries, monkhood). One chapter (p. 241-315) presents a general description of religion, and this is very useful for it is very similar to that of Bhutan. Pages 14-15 give a general history of Bhutan. The book was first published in Calcutta in 1894.

32   Bhutan.
Dehradun, India: Survey of India for the Ministry of External Affairs, Government of India, 1972.
This coloured map (88 × 156 cm) on a scale of 1 : 7,500,000 gives a graphic representation of Bhutan and its environs (metalled roads, cart tracks, bridges, rivers, streams, towns, villages, temples, international boundaries, post offices and telegraph offices). There is also an index to provinces of Bhutan.

33   Bhutan, G.S.G.S. 4948. Sheet E 3.
London: Director of Military Survey, Ministry of Defence, 1978.
A coloured wall map (89 × 121 cm) on a scale of 1 : 300,000 which provides a graphic representation of Bhutan's political boundaries, its physical aspects and its major communications.

34   Bhutan: landcover, soil and water reflections from Landsat imagery (edge-enhanced false-color composites).
Washington DC: World Bank, 1982.
This colour Landsat map (78 × 135 cm) on a scale of 1 : 250,000 shows settlements, communications, grid and overprint. It is a location map, showing Landsat scenes and giving the dates of images used.

9

Geography and Geology. Maps, atlases and gazetteers

35 **Bhutan.**
Friederike Diefenbacher unter Betreuung von [under the supervision of] Professor Ch. Hermann. Karlsruhe, West Germany: Fachhochschule, 1988.

This coloured topographical sketch map (31 × 58 cm) on a scale of 1 : 600,000 shows international boundaries, roads under construction, asphalted roads, cart tracks, paths, Thimphu and Paro inhabitants, widely spread settlements, the capital, districts, airfield, temples, and mountain heights in metres.

36 **Fully annotated atlas of South Asia.**
Ashok K. Dutt, M. Margaret Geib. London: Westview, 1987. 231p. maps, bibliog.

The atlas covers India, Pakistan, Bangladesh, Nepal, Sri Lanka and Bhutan. Bhutan, which may be physically divided into three regions (the Great Himalayas, the Middle Himalayas, and the Duars plains), is located in mountains between the China-ruled Tibetan plateau and the Indian states of Sikkim, West Bengal, Assam, and the union territory of Arunachal Pradesh. On pages 217-24 there are black-and-white line maps of Bhutan showing physical settings, administrative divisions, grain crops, land use (for rice, maize, wheat, barley, and millet), density of population, development planning and roads. All maps contain background information for map users.

37 **Bhutan Himalaya.**
Augusto Gansser, Eduard Imhof. Zurich: Swiss Foundation for Alpine Research, [n.d.].

This is a colour topographical map (40 × 60 cm) on a scale of 1 : 500,000. It bears no date but was most probably published in 1970.

38 **The Imperial gazetteer of India.**
Oxford: Clarendon Press, 1908. new ed. 25 vols.

Pages 154-63 of volume viii present some very useful information on the physical aspects, history, population, agriculture, trade, communication, and the administration of Bhutan in the nineteenth century.

39 **India: official standard names approved by the United States Board on Geographic Names.**
Washington, DC: Division of Geography, Department of the Interior, April 1952. 2 vols.

The two volumes of this gazetteer contain about 30,650 names: 260 of places and features in Bhutan (vol. 1, pages 1-8). Also included are latitude and longitude, administrative division and location references.

40 **The kingdom of Bhutan.**
Pradyumna P. Karan. Washington, DC: Association of American Geographers, 1965.

A colour map (79 × 137 cm) on a scale of 1 : 253,440, showing communications, settlements (Paro Dzong, Taga Dzong – monasteries), La Pass, bridges, landing area for aeroplanes, fortresses, shrines, rivers, lakes and glaciers. Inset is a reliability diagram. There is also an index map showing the location of Bhutan. A map supplement no. 5 is contained in *Annals of the Association of American Geographers*, vol. 55, no. 4 for December 1965.

41   **A historical atlas of South Asia.**
Edited by Joseph E. Schwartzberg, with the collaboration of Shiva Gopal Bajpai, Raj B. Mathur (et al.).   Chicago; London: University of Chicago Press, 1978. 352p. maps. bibliog. (Association for Asian Studies Reference Series, no. 2).

In this detailed and comprehensive cartographic record of the history and culture of South Asia from prehistory to the modern times, there are about forty-five different pages on Bhutan which provide information on primary political units, confederacies, independent states, dependencies, peoples (nation, tribes, castes, clans) and dynasties.

42   **Place and river-names in the Darjiling district and Sikkim.**
Lawrence Austine Waddell.   *Journal of the Asiatic Society of Bengal*, vol. 60, part 1 (1891), p. 53-77.

Waddell discusses the languages and the people inhabiting Sikkim. He covers the names of rivers, mountains, passes, monasteries, and villages in Lepcha, Bhotia, Nepali, Pharia and Bengali. For some names etymological definitions and meanings are given. Bhotia is another name for the Bhutani of Bhutan.

Travel guides

43   **Hill resorts of India, Nepal and Bhutan: a travellers' guide.**
Edited by A. C. Agarwal, A. C. Khanna, K. K. Sawhney, S. R. Vasist, Miss Kavita.   New Delhi: Nest & Wings (India), 1977. 7th ed. 23 parts (of various pagination) bound in one.

The lure of the Himalayas continues to fascinate and attract people from all over the world. This book is very useful to tourists visiting India, Nepal, Bhutan, and Ladakh. The book is divided into 23 sections, of which Section 22 (pages 50-64) includes a brief history and describes the beauty of Bhutan, its places of history, culture, arts, mediaeval dzongs or baronial castles, postage stamps and coins (silver, copper and gold). Information about package tours run by the Tourist Department of Bhutan is also given.

44   **Tourist guide to Darjeeling, Sikkim and Bhutan, Kalimpong and Mirik: a travellers' guide.**
Edited by A. P. Agarwala.   New Delhi: Nest & Wings (India), 1982. 101p.

This guide is intended for the tourist who has very little time to read and who wishes to know about the land, history, culture, places of interest and transport facilities. Pages 89-101 are on Bhutan.

Geography and Geology. Travel guides

45 **Let's visit Bhutan.**
Aung San Suu Kyi. London: Burke, 1985. 96p.
This book provides information on the social life and customs of the people of Bhutan. Not only does it give the facts about religion, religious and hereditary monarchs, daily life, fortresses and festivals, but there are also 45 photographs, mostly in colour, depicting the everyday life of the people. Some information on art, paintings and sculpture is also included: the subjects are always of a religious nature, and the finest examples of architecture are to be seen in the structure of dzongs (monasteries) and temples. This publication is meant for children, but it is also quite useful for people visiting Bhutan.

46 **Bhutan the Himalayan paradise.**
Dilip Bhattacharyya. New Delhi: Oxford & IBH, 1975. 62p. map.
Though short, this is a good tourist guide, providing sufficient information about the people, the history of Bhutan, its climate, transport and communications, language, art and architecture, the system of government, popular places of interest and some Bhutanese vocabulary in Roman characters with English translations. There is also a tourist guide map with 32 illustrations including photographs (some of which are in colour) and free-hand sketches.

47 **Himalaya: Kaachmir, Ladakh, Nordindische Täler, Nepal, Sikkim, Bhutan.** (Himalaya: Kashmir, Ladakh, North Indian valleys, Nepal, Sikkim, Bhutan.)
Manfred Gerner. Pforzheim, West Germany: Goldstadtverlag, 1976. 363p. maps. bibliog.
This is a useful handbook for visitors to Bhutan who want to see the tourist attractions in the country. Between pages 317 and 344, each place worthy of a visit is described, together with information on religion, society, culture, and climate of the country. The text is in German.

48 **The Himalayan kingdoms Nepal, Bhutan and Sikkim.**
Bob Gibbons, Bob Ashford. London: Batsford, 1983. 157p. maps. bibliog.
This book consists of descriptions of Nepal, Bhutan and Sikkim, all with photographs. Pages 114 to 141 describe Bhutan as a most remote and beautiful land which, since 1974, has opened its doors to a few thousand foreign travellers each year. A brief and handy guide for travellers who want to know about Bhutan, its people, history, religion, industry, agriculture, places worth visiting, and the achievements of modern Bhutan from 1950 to 1983.

49 **Nepal, Sikkim and Bhutan: Himalayan kingdoms in pictures.**
Eugene Gordon. New York: Sterling; London and Sydney: Oak Tree Press, 1972. 64p. (Visual Geography Series).
This is a fairly brief travel guide to the Himalayan states. Bhutan has an area of about 19,305 square miles and a population of about 1,232,000 people. The information on Bhutan covers four pages and concerns its people, economy, history, and government. Each article is illustrated by photographs taken by the author.

50 **Bhutan.**
Pietro Francesco Mele. New York: Paragon Book Gallery, 1982. 58p.
A beautifully illustrated guide for travellers about the myth, mystery and beauty of the country. There is a short introduction to the history and geography of Bhutan, together with 49 colour photographs depicting such varied topics as Himalayan jungles, Bhutanese architecture in the Paro valley, and Bhutanese bathing in a small river heated by hot stones; monasteries, archery, government officials and other people of Bhutan; the museum, the Royal palace together with its architectural details, Lamas, sacred dancers, and dancers wearing masks against evil spirits. The pages in the book are not numbered.

51 **Where the Gods are mountains: three years among the people of the Himalayas.**
René von Nebesky-Wojkowitz, translated from the German by Michael Bullock. London: Weidenfeld and Nicolson, 1956. 265p.
The author travelled from Calcutta to the Himalayan states of Sikkim, Darjeeling and Bhutan between 1950 and 1953. On pages 162-8 he describes his journey and his impressions of Bhutan, commenting in particular on his meeting with the present King and Queen of Bhutan and their Western lifestyle and liking for Western music. He also provides a partial guide to early travellers' accounts with a survey of European visitors to Bhutan from Portugal and Britain.

52 **India: a handbook of travel.**
P. B. Roy. Narendrapur, India: Saturday Mail Publications, 1988. 6th enlarged ed. 503p.
This guide, which is extremely readable and very useful to foreign travellers, was first published in 1954 and has abundant information on travel in India. Pages 141-6 provide the reader with an outline of Bhutan's ancient culture and past and present history, Roy also describes the land, the people, tourism, transport, and visa requirements.

53 **Bhutan: a kingdom of the Eastern Himalayas.**
Photographs by Guy van Strydonck, texts by Françoise Pommaret-Imaeda, Yoshiro Imaeda, English translation by Ian Noble. London: Serindia, 1984. 175p. map. bibliog.
The book provides a beautifully illustrated guide on many varied subjects including Bhutan's social, economic and political institutions, its religion, and its philosophy of life which has imparted stability and strength to the Bhutanese people from ancient times. There are 113 photographs which capture the natural beauty, rhythm of life, peace and harmony, and the essence of the country. This book is intended for travellers; the French edition was published in Geneva in 1984.

54 **Trekker's guide to the Himalaya and Karakoram.**
Hugh Swift, with additional material by Rodney Jackson, Charles Gay, Helena Norberg-Hodge, Milan W. Melvin, John H. Mock. San Francisco, California: Sierra Club Books, 1982. 342p. maps. bibliog.
The bulk of this guide covers the mountainous areas of Pakistan (Chitral, Gilgit and Baltistan) and India (Kashmir, Ladakh, Himachal Pradesh and Garhwal), but it also describes central and eastern Nepal, with brief sections on Sikkim and Bhutan (pages

13

239-66). In Bhutan every group, whether tour or trek, is escorted by a trained guide of the Bhutan Travel Agency. As of 1981, only a 50-mile-wide corridor in the western part of Bhutan had been opened to visiting or trekking. The longest and most interesting of the guided treks offered, is between Paro Dzong and Thimpu by way of the base of Mount Homolhari (23,997 ft), on the border with Tibet.

55   **Trekking in Nepal, West Tibet, and Bhutan.**
     Hugh Swift, with additional material by Charles Gay, Peter H. Hackett, M. D. Rodney Jackson, Millan M. Melvin.   London; Sydney; Auckland; Toronto: Hodder & Stoughton, 1989. 360p. maps.

This guide is a completely revised, updated, and expanded edition of the best single-volume book available on trekking in this beautiful area, an area which is full of ice-crowned peaks, sequestered valleys, glaciated passes, dense forests, plunging rivers, snow-fed lakes, and exotic towns and peoples. It covers all the major routes and destinations, including the principal hiking routes in Bhutan and the trail to the base of Chomolhari. The authors also include practical advice on clothing, equipment lists, expense estimates, documents, permits, and immunizations.

56   **Bhutan – Fürstenstaat am Götterthron.** (Bhutan – a princely state on the throne of the gods.)
     Ninon Vellis, Armin Haab.   Gütersloh, West Germany: Sigbert Mohn, 1961. 176p. maps. bibliog.

There is a good deal of information on both the country of Bhutan and its people. The book is lavishly illustrated with photographs, not to be found in other books, and is an excellent example of a tourist guide.

Travellers' accounts

57   **Travels in Bhutan.**
     F. M. Bailey.   *Journal of the Royal Central Asian Society*, vol. 17, no. 1 (1930), p. 206-20.

This was the lecture given by Lieutenant-Colonel Bailey, CIE, to the Central Asian Society on 12 March 1930. The author had recently been to Bhutan, where he was able to make a film; it was the first ever made of that country, and he showed it during his lecture. The lecture covered the whole area of the country and its geographical position; religious history; British relations with Bhutan from 1774 to 1922; internal disturbances in Bhutan; the characteristics of the people and their housing conditions; and sundry other topics such as the life of a chief, fauna and flora, the weaving of silk, Bhutanese hospitality, and architecture.

58   **Lepcha land or six weeks in the Sikkim Himalayas: with a map showing route, and 106 illustrations.**
      Florence Donaldson.   London: Sampson Low Marston, 1900. 213p.
In this exciting tale of travel and adventure in Sikkim Florence Donaldson recounts her journey to the Jelep La Pass in 1891, together with a few necessary remarks on the history of different races found in Sikkim. Although the author does not discuss the Lepchas of Bhutan, this book does provide considerable general information about Lepchas, a Mongolian tribe forming a large part of the population of Sikkim, and some of Bhutan and Darjeeling. The photographs and the text indicate the extreme primitiveness of the people and the problems faced by them. Lepcha physiognomy is markedly Mongolian: short stature – about five feet tall, face broad and flat, depressed nose, oblique eyes, beardless chin, and olive skin. The Lepchas have no class distinctions and are an honest, timid and peaceful people.

59   **Journal of travels in Assam, Burma, Bootan, Afghanistan and the neighbouring countries.**
      William Griffith.   Calcutta: Bishop's College Press, 1847. 529p.
The journal describes the social, religious and curious customs of the people. The primitive state of the society and the influence of both the priests and monks on the general public in Bhutan is well known, but the journal suffers from an obsession with occidental superiority and high tone. Griffith's observations on Bhutanese social, religious and political institutions are fallacious, but his account of the zoology and botany of the country is the first of its kind. The work was reprinted in India in 1971.

60   **Report on the explorations in Sikkim, Bhutan and Tibet.**
      Lama Serap Gyatsho, [Explorer] K. P., [Lama] V. G., [Explorer]
      R. N., [Explorer] P. A.   Dehra Dun, India: Trigonometrical Branch,
      Survey of India, 1889, p. 37-57.
This is a report on the explorations of Lama Serap Gyatsho (1856-68), Explorer K. P. (1880-84), Lama V. G. (1883), Explorer R. N. (1885-86), and Explorer P. A. (1885-86) in Sikkim, Bhutan and Tibet. This account of the explorations in Bhutan was compiled by G. W. E. Atkinson, from information verbally communicated to him by the explorer R. N. from the vernacular notes made in the course of his travels in 1885-86. His information was also used in the preparation of the map of Bhutan published in 1907. It is a very interesting account of the hard work of five different explorers between 1856 and 1886.

61   **Dreams of the peaceful dragon: a journey through Bhutan.**
      Katie Hickman.   London: Gollancz, 1987. 192p. map.
This travel account describes how Katie Hickman reached Bhutan and met both the Royal family and many of the ordinary Bhutanese people. The people are mostly vegetarians and extremely religious. The work also describes the massive state monasteries, together with a note on the hard life led by the people, and appreciates the fact that everything the people use and consume, is actually made by themselves. The author also tells of her experience of travelling at an altitude of 8,000 to 14,000 ft, for about ten to twelve hours a day, and meeting innocent and ignorant people who have never before met any foreigners.

62 **The gates of Thibet.**
J. A. H. Louis. Delhi: Vivek, 1972. 181p.
This book contains much information on religion and history, in addition to the author's general observations as a traveller in British Bhutan (pages 16-24). He describes its forest produce, roads, suspension bridges, and orange groves. The British–Bhutan treaty of 1865 is also included. The book was first published in Calcutta – by the Catholic Orphan Press in 1894 – under the title of *The Gates of Thibet: a bird's eye view of independent Sikkim, British Bhootan, and the Dooars, as a Doorga Poojah Trip.*

63 **John Marshall in India: notes and observations in Bengal, 1668-1672.**
John Marshall. London: Oxford University Press, 1927. 471p.
Marshall provides an account of his travels to Patna, Narainpur, Hooghly, Kashmir, Delhi, Nepal, Bhutan, China and Japan. He describes geographical features, religion, philosophy, ascetics, astrology, medicine, diseases, folklore, and the laws and languages of the areas covered during his travels.

64 **The Indian Alps, and how we crossed them; being a narrative of two years residence in the Eastern Himalaya and two months tour into the interior, by a Lady Pioneer (pseud.)**
Nina-Elizabeth Mazuchelli. London: Longmans Green, 1876. 612p. map.
The author gives a detailed account of her journey from India to Darjeeling, Bhutan and the Eastern Himalayas, together with notes on scenery, forests, social life of the people, and Buddhist monks.

65 **A journey in Bhutan.**
C. J. Morris. *Geographical Journal*, vol. 86 (1935), p. 201-15.
A charmingly written account of a journey to Bhutan, its physical features, history, people, and their customs. There are occasional references to Sikkim in this article.

66 **Bhutan: land of hidden treasures.**
Text by Blanche C. Olschak, photography by Ursula and Augusto Gansser. London: George Allen & Unwin, 1971. 63p.
This volume provides a brief description of Bhutanese religion, customs, and sociology. There are fifty-seven articles, each covering a page or so. Subjects covered include the mask dances, a mountain goddess, guest dancers, a festival in the valley of the swans, white stupas, the temple of the broken bell, sword dance, a fortress (Simthoka Dzong), a lotus-grove monastery (Patshalling Gompa), and an iron bridge. The book largely refers to the day-to-day living traditions of Bhutan. The second part of the book contains eighty illustrations supporting the text and showing Bhutanese people, monasteries, mountains, and various other objects of interest.

67   **The dragon kingdom: images of Bhutan.**
Text by Blanche Christine Olschak, translated from the German by
Michael H. Kohn, photographs by Ursula Markus-Gansser, Augusto
Gansser.   Boston, Massachusetts: Shambhala, 1988. 104p. map.

Blanche Olschak is a specialist in the early history of Central Asia and the Himalayan
regions, while Ursula Markus-Gansser is a freelance photographer and Augusto
Gansser is a professor of geology. Olschak and Markus-Gansser recently made a three-
month excursion by caravan through Bhutan, observing its magnificent landscapes, its
monastic and village life, and its colourful festivals and dances. The book contains
articles on: cliff monasteries and castles; Mahayana Buddhism; the magic dance of
Bhutan; the coronation of the youngest king in the world; and a graphic description of
the authors' journey into the dragon country. It is beautifully illustrated with colour
photographs.

68   **Lords and Lamas: a solitary expedition across the secret Himalayan
kingdom of Bhutan.**
Michel Peissel.   London: Heinemann, 1970. 180p. map.

This is an eye-witness account of Peissel's journey into this primitive and most
beautiful land where some people have never seen a car or heard a radio and are
ignorant of many other things which a person in the West would think it normal to
possess. The author, a French national, speaks fluent Tibetan and describes the social
patterns of Bhutan, artistic skills, his meeting and dinner with the Queen of Bhutan,
and a monastery where the King shared his rule with the reincarnated Lama. The
author recollects that in 1968 – when he visited the country – it had started the intricate
process of evolution and modernization.

69   **The view of Hindoostan.**
Thomas Pennant.   London: Printed by Henry Hughes, 1798-1800.
4 vols.

Volume 1 (Western India), vol. 2 (Eastern Hindustan), vol. 3 (View of India, China
and Japan) and vol. 4 (The view of Malayan isles) combine to provide a classic account
of the author's travels to the south, east and west of India, as well as to Sri Lanka,
Nepal, and Bhutan. The books describe the social life of the people and the author's
impressions of the countries visited. It is an account which contains some interesting
material and a useful description of Bhutan.

70   **Himalayan Bhutan, Sikkim and Tibet.**
Earl of Ronaldshay.   Delhi: Ess Ess Publications, 1977. 267p.

These countries contain some of the most impressive mountain scenery in the world,
and even if their interest lay solely in their physical characteristics, they would be
worthy of the homage of the most blasé traveller. This book is a deep and absorbing
study of Bhutan and contains a comprehensive examination of the folk culture and
religion of the people of the area. It is a narrative of travel in somewhat out-of-the-way
locations of great natural charm, and among people whose strange characteristics give
them an unusual interest. The book, which was first published in 1920, is complete in
itself and is intelligible without reference to others of its companion volumes.

71 **Lands of the thunderbolt: Sikhim, Chumbi and Bhutan.**
Earl of Ronaldshay.   London: Constable, 1923. 267p. map.
This is a travel account of the countries situated in the Eastern Himalayas on the
northern borders of Bengal. The subjects covered include religion, the life of Buddha,
various aspects of Buddhism, Lamaism in practice, and some of the most impressive
mountain scenery in the world. On the subject of Bhutan itself, the author briefly gives
the history of how in 747 AD Guru Padma Sambhava became the most powerful person
in the land by teaching people Buddhism as known in Tibet. One of the chief emblems
of the Guru's might was the Vajrah, or the symbol of the thunderbolt of Indira, a
Hindu God. Pages 197-219 of the book covers Bhutan's relations with the British
government from 1772 to 1911.

72 **The Dragon kingdom: journeys through Bhutan.**
E. A. Vas.   New Delhi: Lancer International, 1986. 372p. map. bibliog.
The author visited Bhutan several times between 1961 and 1985. Apart from describing
his journeys, the country and the people he met, Lieutenant-General Vas has
interspersed his fascinating narrative with background information about the history
and geography of Bhutan, so that certain events may be understood in their proper
perspective. The author is an amateur naturalist: he saw many rare birds and animals
and kept notes on the flora and fauna, and those observations are also woven into his
account. A list of the principal animals and birds to be found in Bhutan is included in
an appendix.

73 **Among the Himalayas.**
Lawrence Austine Waddell.   London: Constable, 1899. 452p.
This book basically provides a descriptive account of journeys throughout the
Himalayan states, and especially Sikkim, for over a decade. On pages 239-54 there is a
good account of the chiefs of Bhutan, the social life of its people, and its forts.

Flora and Fauna

74 **Field guide to the birds of the Eastern Himalayas.**
Salim Ali.   Delhi: Oxford University Press, 1977. 265p.
The Eastern Himalayas includes Bhutan, the Indian state of Sikkim and Arunachal
Pradesh. The Duars of Assam and Bengal have been included for the sake of
completeness, since many of the birds who normally live at greater heights descend to
them to spend the winter months. There are 536 birds described in the book, and 366
of them are illustrated in colour. The status and habitats of the birds are also
mentioned. For details of the overall range, within the subcontinent and beyond,
reference should be made to the *Handbook of the birds of India and Pakistan* by the
same author (q.v.).

75 **Handbook of the birds of India and Pakistan together with those of
Bangladesh, Nepal, Bhutan and Sri Lanka.**
Salim Ali, S. Dillon Ripley.   Bombay; London; New York; Oxford
University Press, 1969. 10 vols. maps. bibliog.
This is a well-written and well-illustrated guide by the leading authorities on the life
history, behaviour, and biogeography of the birds of South Asia.

76 **The large and small game of Bengal and the North Western provinces of
India.**
John Henry Baldwin.   London: Kegan Paul, Trench, 1883. 2nd ed.
380p.
The author describes the general characteristics of the wildlife (wild buffalo, tiger,
panther, leopard, black bear, hyena, pheasant, quail, snow partridge, bustard, cobra,
wood snipe, wild duck and hare) he encountered during his journeys in Bengal,
Assam, Himalaya, Bhutan, Tibet, Simla and Jhansi. He also provides information on
the hunting and shooting of some of the birds and animals.

Flora and Fauna

77 **Notes on some birds in Mr. Mandelli's collection from Sikkim, Bhutan, and Tibet.**
William T. Blanford. *Stray Feathers*, V (1877), p. 482-7.
A detailed description is given of birds recently procured from these countries by Mandelli.

78 **A plant collector in Bhutan.**
R. E. Cooper. *Scottish Geographical Magazine*, vol. 58, no. 1 (March 1942), p. 9-15.
The author describes his journeys in Bhutan – from June to November 1940 and from April to October 1941 – in search of plants. The article provides an account of the most important species in relation to their habitat, rather than a comprehensive listing. The plants which carry the blossoms are very small and often the flowers themselves are very tiny, but the sheer quantity of plants gives the fine colour effect. He mentions one new plant which he found; it proved to be a species of *Lobelia*, and his was the first and only record of it, not only in the Himalayas, but in Asia, Europe or North America.

79 **Wild India: the wildlife and scenery of India and Nepal.**
Gerald Cubbit, Guy Mountfort. London: William Collins, 1985. 208p. map.
This standard reference work covers: geography and climate; vegetation and the monsoon; wildlife; the Himalayas; the Indo-gangetic plain and the Deccan. This book has a foreword by HRH The Duke of Edinburgh KT, KG and it is dedicated to Mrs Indira Gandhi, whose personal interest in the production of this book was an inspiration to the authors. Pages 84, 85 and 88 describe a beautiful golden monkey from the Bhutan Manas Reserve. The book has extremely beautiful pictures and is well illustrated.

80 **The quest for flowers: the plant explorations of Frank Ludlow and George Sherriff told from their diaries and other occasional writings.**
Harold R. Fletcher. Edinburgh: Edinburgh University Press, 1975. 363p.
The volume provides a detailed account of Ludlow and Sheriff's plant-hunting expedition in south-eastern Tibet. It not only describes some of the more interesting plants collected, but also gives some impression of the country and of the hazards of plant-collecting in the region. It includes the botanical expeditions of 1933 – to the pass of the flowers in North East Bhutan; 1934 – Tibet and East Bhutan; 1937 – to the Black mountains of Central Bhutan; and 1949 – temperate and alpine Bhutan. There are 361 plates and a botanical index to plants.

81 **Tales of our grand father, or India since 1856.**
L. J. H. Grey. London: Smith, Elder, 1912. 305p.
Colonel Grey describes wildlife in Assam, Bhutan and Bahalwalpur, and provides a general introduction to the social life and caste system, as well as to dances and sports. Army and shooting games are also included.

82 **Himalayan journals or notes of a naturalist in Bengal, the Sikkim and Nepal Himalayas, the Khasia mountains, &c.**
Joseph Dalton Hooker. London: Ward, Lock, 1905. 574p. maps.
In this work Hooker's comparison of the newly discovered plants with those already known in other parts of the world, has led to many novel conclusions as to the laws governing the distribution of plants over the earth's surface. Hooker was a renowned botanist, and the area which he explored in 1849 had never been approached by any European. The journal provides us with a fascinating account of the nature of the Duar country (Bhutan) against the background of Himalayan geography. There are about ninety illustrations in the text.

83 **Travels in Peru and India; while superintending the collection of chinchona plants and seeds in South America and their introduction into India.**
Clements R. Markham. London: John Murray, 1862. 572p. maps.
This is a general sketch of southern India (Malabar, Madura, Trichinopoly [Tiruchirapalli], Mysore, Coorg and Deccan), together with notes on population, gardens, plantations, cultivation, soil, climate and flora. Particular attention is given to chinchona cultivation in Bhutan, Sikkim and Ceylon.

84 **Mountain development: challenges and opportunities.**
Kathmandu: International Centre for Integrated Mountain Development, 1984. 12p.
This volume – the Proceedings of the first International Symposium and Inauguration of the International Centre for Integrated Mountain Development, held on 1-5 December 1983 in Kathmandu, Nepal – records only the speeches of distinguished guests and the technical presentations by the expert delegates. Pages 16-17 consist of a statement by C. Dorji of Bhutan on its population, forests, land use, vegetation, animal husbandry, and mountainous environment.

85 **Forest types of India, Nepal and Bhutan.**
S. S. Negi. Delhi: Periodical Expert Book Agency, 1989. 322p.
This is the only book which deals with the state-by-state distribution of forest types in India. Dr Negi also gives for the first time a brief description of the forest types of Nepal and Bhutan. Part three of the book (p. 298-320) deals with the forests of Bhutan which are very diverse both in nature and composition: they range from tropical and sub-tropical hardwood forests to alpine pastures and meadows. A brief introduction to the topography and the climate of Bhutan is followed by a detailed classification into forest types, and, finally, by distribution lists and altitude ranges for specific trees. This information is very useful for foresters, botanists, naturalists and even the layman who is interested in the unique forest wealth of India.

86 **Flowers of the Himalaya.**
Oleg Polunin, Adam Stainton. Oxford: Oxford University Press, 1984. 580p. map.
This provides a very useful reference work, heavily based on the work of earlier botanists and collectors. Plants are treated by family, with the species arranged in alphabetical order within each family section. A note on countries, states and

Flora and Fauna

geographical divisions which indicate distribution of species is given. There are about 360 line drawings and about 128 pages of colour illustrations of flowers. Some technical terms are used and a glossary of these is provided.

87   **India's wildlife and wildlife reserves.**
   B. Seshadri.   London: Oriental University Press, 1986. 215p.

This book was commissioned by the publisher to fill a gap in Indian wildlife literature. The main aim of the guide is to introduce readers to the wildlife community and the more important reserves. Relevant to Bhutan are pages 109-11, on the Manas Tiger Reserve. The guide is illustrated and attractively produced, and also provides practical information on means of travel, accommodation, the best time of the year to visit, and whom to contact for further information.

88   **The riddles of the Tsangpo gorges.**
   Francis Kingdon Ward.   London: Edward Arnold, 1926. 324p. map.

Professor Ward was an eminent botanist and he made an exhaustive survey of the Himalayan area where India, Burma and China meet. He worked on the distribution of the vegetation in the Himalayas, and without his achievements our knowledge of the botany of the area would be very scant indeed. In this book he provides a general geographical description of Tibet and his report of the 1924-25 expedition, from Darjeeling to Kalimpong and through Sikkim to Bhutan and back to India. This treatise includes the description of plants and their habitats, as well as remarks on hill tribes and Tibetans in general. An index of plants, photographs, and a route map are also included.

History

General

89 **State of historical research in the Himalayan region.**
Shyam K. Bhurtel, Ramesh Dhungel. In: *Preparatory workshop on Himalayan studies*, 23-24 September 1984, edited by Ananda Shrestha. Kathmandu: Centre for Nepal and Asian Studies, [n.d.], p. 17-33.
The author provides a brief survey of work done on the Himalayan region, focusing particularly on Nepal, Bhutan, Sikkim, Kashmir and Tibet. There is a bibliography of about 100 items.

90 **A cultural history of Bhutan.**
B. Chakravarti. Chittaranjan, India: Hilltop Publishers, 1980-81.
2nd ed. 2 vols. bibliog.
Bhutan can be regarded as one of the best repositories of ancient culture, and the author has done well to trace its cultural history from prehistoric times to 1980. Volume 1 covers 400 BC to 747 AD, and Volume 2 from 747 AD to 1980. Archaeology is the primary source for the study of prehistory, but there are no excavations in Bhutan and so the book is based on a study of its linguistics, legends, ethnography, ethnology, geography, geology, physical and cultural anthropology, folklore, oral traditions, religion, theology, and cosmology. There are some gaps in these accounts, but they are likely to promote future research to make our knowledge more comprehensive. The chapter on religious and cultural syncretism will go a long way towards helping the students of southern Bhutan, most of whom are Nepali Hindus, to perceive the interrelation between the Hinduism they practise and the Drukpa Kargyu Buddhism practised by their fellow Bhutanese people in central and northern Bhutan. The book's contribution to a deeper understanding of the two religions should lead to greater religious tolerance and syncretism, a situation which will, in turn, be conducive to the national integration of Bhutan. The information given is authentic because of

the author's association with the general mass of Bhutanese people, and his knowledge of their language, customs and manners.

91 **Bhutan, yesterday and today.**
Peter Collister. *Asian Affairs*, vol. 19, no. 3 (1988), p. 298-305.

The author describes briefly the political history of Bhutan from the mid-16th century to the 1980s. Ngawang Namgyal founded Bhutan in 1639 following a successful revolt from Tibetan rule. Subsequently, although a royal family continued nominal rule, the Chinese emperor exercised secular control over Bhutan for several centuries until the British took over this task in the 19th century. In 1949 India agreed to look after the external affairs and the economic development of Bhutan.

92 **The Dragon country: the general history of Bhutan.**
Nirmala Das. Bombay: Orient Longman, 1974. 99p.

The book is divided into two parts. The first deals with the cultural and social history of Bhutan, Buddhist influence from Tibet, Bhutan-British relations, and Indo-Bhutan relations both during British rule and also with post-independent India. The second part deals entirely with the history of dzongs (administrative centres) and monasteries – both institutions which occupy such an important place in the life of Bhutanese people. This is a useful book for both serious scholars and the general reader.

93 **The coronation of a young King reflects the colorful history of Bhutan in ancient days.**
Ernest Haas. *Smithsonian*, vol. 5, no. 6 (1974), p. 53-63.

The author gives a very good description of the coronation of the teenage absolute monarch (Jigme Singye Wangchuck) on 2 June 1974 in the Himalayan kingdom of Bhutan. On this spectacular occasion the last of the 'forbidden kingdoms' opened its doors to 150 foreign dignitaries. The teenage king declared that Bhutan must soon achieve economic self-reliance. Some photographs are included with the text.

94 **History of Bhutan: land of the peaceful dragon.**
Bikrama Jit Hasrat. Thimphu: Education Department, 1980. 242p. map. bibliog.

Professor B. J. Hasrat, a well-known historian on the Himalayan region, was commissioned by the Royal Government of Bhutan to write this book outlining Bhutan's history from ancient times. Apart from the socio-political and religious ideas which have shaped Bhutan's history, he has also dealt with the rich and diverse customs, traditions and achievements in the field of literature, art, archaeology, culture and religion. British and Indian relations with Bhutan are based on the official records of the British and Indian governments. This book is of great interest both to the general reader and also to students of Bhutan's history in particular.

95 **Sikkim und Bhutan: Die verfassungsgeschichtliche und politische Entwicklung der indischen Himalaya-Protektorate.** (Sikkim and Bhutan: the constitutional history and political development of the Indian Himalayan protectorate.)
Hellmuth Hecker. Frankfurt, West Germany: Alfred Metzner, 1970. 73p. bibliog.

This German work is a welcome addition to the literature of the less well known Himalayan kingdoms of Bhutan and Sikkim, dealing with the history, development, political situation and administration of the countries. The text of the peace treaty signed between the British Government and the Government of Bhutan on 11 November 1865, along with the text of the peace treaty between the Government of India and the Government of Bhutan signed on 8 August 1949, are also mentioned.

96 **Institutional achievements and the process of nation-building in Bhutan.**
R. C. Mishra. In: *The Himalayas: profiles of modernisation and adaptation*, edited by S. K. Chaube. New Delhi: Sterling, 1985, p. 196-209.

This [seventeenth] chapter covers the role of the monarchy in the processes of nation-building from the seventeenth century to modern times. It describes the seventeenth-century internal dissensions among major heads of sub-regions and how the topography of Bhutan prevented any outside interference in maintaining its independent status. The other institutions that owe their existence to the institution of monarchy are: the Tshogdu (Legislative Assembly), which was established in 1953; the Independent Bhutanese Church established in the 1960s by appointment of a High Priest of Bhutan; Ladoi Chopdah (the Royal Council), established in 1965; the Bhutanese judiciary; the constitution of Bhutan; the Bank of Bhutan, established in 1968. The roles of these institutions are described, together with the procedure for the administration of justice, and the economic development programmes from 1961 onwards.

97 **Behind Bhutan's throne.**
Tooshar Pandit. *Eastern World*, vol. 18, no. 10 (Nov. 1964), p. 7-9.

This article provides a brief political history of Bhutan from the ninth century – when the Tibetans assumed power in Bhutan by defeating the Hindu kings of the Madra dynasty – up to 1964. There is also a brief introduction to the circumstances leading to the assassination of the Prime Minister of Bhutan (Jigme Dorjee) on 5 April 1964, and the economic development in the country in relation to the First Five-Year Development Plan which started in 1961.

98 **Les royaumes de l'Himalaya. Édition française établie par Bernard Blanc.** (The kingdoms of the Himalaya. French edition by Bernard Blanc.)
Michel Peissel. Barbizon, France: Pierre Bordas et fils, 1986. 226p. maps.

On pages 187-90 there is a straightforward account of the history and civilization of Bhutan from 650 to 1964.

99 Land of the peaceful dragon: past and present – brief history.
Lopon Pemala. *Asian Culture*, vol. 35 (Summer/Autumn 1983), p. 1-7.

The history of Bhutan from 1500 BC to 1982 is traced in this article. The account emphasizes the British period and its political events and movements. There is some information on social and economic conditions and social change in the state. A chronological table from 600 AD to 1982 is also provided at the end of the article.

100 Modern Bhutan.
Ram Rahul. Delhi: Vikas, 1971. 173p. map. bibliog.

A survey of the history of Bhutan from about 650 AD to 1907, when the present line of kings began. It contains a list of the kings, rulers and dignitaries of Bhutan from 1594 to 1971, the system of government, its structure and functioning, the influence of Buddhism on the life and culture of the people, and Bhutan's foreign relations with India and China. There is also a chronology of Bhutan from 1616 to 1971, and the whole work is a reliable and useful study of Bhutanese people. The author, who is an Indian specialist on the Himalayan states, claims that it is the first book of its kind on Bhutan.

101 Royal Bhutan.
Ram Rahul. New Delhi: ABC Publishing, 1983. 85p. bibliog.

Rahul provides a short political history of Bhutan's monarchy in this book which is intended for the general reader and which is particularly good for anyone interested in a chronological study of Bhutan's history. He deals especially with the condition of Bhutan's government from 1862 to 1972, but also attempts to study the efforts made by His Majesty King Jigme Singye Wangchuck, from 1955 onwards, to adopt or elaborate the existing administrative structure, in order to achieve more competent conduct by his government, and thus provide a better service for the people of Bhutan.

102 The changing Bhutan.
Laxman Singh Rathore. New Delhi: Jain Brothers, 1973. 168p. bibliog.

Bhutan provides abundant material for researchers in the fields of geography, sociology, economics, history and political science, and in this study the author examines all the important aspects of Bhutanese social life, as well as some recent developments in the political and constitutional set-up of Bhutan. The history, politics and foreign relations of Bhutan have received special attention in this book, but it also includes an examination of the reforms and process of change in the country, and a summary of the problems and challenges that it still faces.

103 Bhutan: historical survey.
Hari Saran. In: *India's Northern security (including China, Nepal and Bhutan),* edited by Gautam Sharma, K. S. Nagar. New Delhi: Reliance Publishing, 1986, p. 201-16.

The author gives a brief and general account of the history of Bhutan from 1616 onwards, and declares that Bhutan was never a protectorate of Tibet – something that China has claimed in recent times, since it took over Tibet. Moreover, Saran says, Bhutan never used any seals from China, nor did it pay any tribute to Tibet or China. The treaty of 1949 between India and Bhutan is included in the appendix. This article is a useful one for the general reader.

104 **Hindustan year-book and who's who.**
Edited by S. Sarkar. Calcutta: M. C. Sarkar and Sons, 1976. 44th ed.
516, 105p.
This is an annual publication on India which consists of two parts but bound into one.
It provides a very good description of the Himalayan kingdom of Bhutan, which is a
semi-independent state and does not belong to the category of an Indian state in the
real sense. In respect of its foreign relations, Bhutan is a protectorate of the
Government of India. Page 81 (in Part 1) and pages 25-6 (in Part 2) both contain brief
and factual information on some historical topics of interest.

Pre-1772

105 **Bhutan: the early history of a Himalayan kingdom.**
Michael Aris. Warminster, England: Aris and Phillips, 1979. 345p.
bibliog.
The author spent five years in Bhutan as a private tutor to the royal family, and this is
a scholarly book based mostly on local sources and on a large number of Tibetan texts,
from both Bhutan and Tibet. In the first place the book is dedicated to mythological
material, arranged in chronological order and with special attention to the ruling
families of the various clans and chieftains into which ancient Bhutan was divided.
Secondly, it describes the development of social and religious institutions from the
tenth to the seventeenth centuries, and dealing mostly with monastic estates in
mediaeval Bhutan. Thirdly, there is a full account of the life of the founder of the
Bhutanese theocratic state, the Zhabs-drung Ngag-dbang-rnam-rgyal (1594-1651), and
lastly, Aris gives the main trends of developments from the eighteenth to the twentieth
centuries, down to the foundation of the secular monarchy in 1907. The book contains
some useful information which cannot be found elsewhere. There are 31 plates,
reproducing objects and buildings of interest. The book concludes with chronological
lists, bibliographies, notes, and useful indexes (Tibetan and General).

106 **Some considerations on the early history of Bhutan.**
Michael Aris. In: *Tibetan studies*, edited by Martin Brauen, Per
Kvaerne. Zurich: Völkerkundemuseum, 1978, p. 5-38. bibliog.
This interesting article arose from a seminar held in Zurich from 26 June to 1 July
1977. It reveals some very important facts and provides considerable information about
the early history of Bhutan. Bhutan is the only country in Asia where Northern
Buddhism survives as the state religion and it has also escaped absorption into China
or India. As a fully independent member of the United Nations, it is trying to preserve
its traditional life embedded in the tenets of Northern Buddhism. It is an extremely
useful article for anyone interested in the earliest history of Bhutan.

107 **Zu den Hintergrunden der Parteinahme Ladakh's für Bhutan im Krieg gegen Lhasa.** (On the background to Ladakh's support for Bhutan in the war against Lhasa.)
Dieter Schuh. In: *Recent research on Ladakh*, edited by Detlef Kantowsky, Reinhard Sander. Munich, West Germany: Weltforum, 1983, p. 37-50.

This chapter provides information on Ladakh's links with Bhutan through their common allegiance to the Brug-pa sect of Buddhism, and Ladakh's consequent support of Bhutan in a war against Tibet in the second half of the seventeenth century.

1772-

108 **Historical documents of Assam and neighbouring states original records in English.**
N. N. Acharyya. New Delhi: Omsons Publications, 1983. 232p.

Acharyya has collected all the original documents which are included in this volume. On the subject of Bhutan, pages 119-38 include the original texts of: articles of a treaty between the Honourable East India Company and the Deva Raja or Raja of Bhutan, 1773; proposals from the Bhutan Deputies for a treaty of peace (17 March 1774); Walter Hamilton's report on Bhutan, 1820; Anglo-Bhutanese treaty of 28 January 1853; Anglo-Bhutan treaty of 1863; and the Assam administration report 1879-80 relating to Anglo-Bhutanese relations.

109 **A collection of treaties, engagements and sunnuds relating to India and neighbouring countries.**
C. U. Aitchison. Calcutta: Superintendent Government Printing, 1909. 4th ed. 13 vols.

Volume 2, pages 285-307, includes a brief historical sketch of Bhutan and also provides the background for the text of the treaties of peace and friendship of 1774, 1844, 1864, 1865 between Bhutan and Great Britain. The proclamation regarding annexation of the Duars, dated 4 July 1866, and the translation of a permit granted by Dharma Raja for the construction of a road in Bhutan, dated 27 February 1904, are also included. Other editions of Aitchison's *Treaties* appeared as follows: 1st edition, 1862; 2nd edition, 1876; 3rd edition, 1892; and 5th edition, 1929.

110 **Views of medieval Bhutan. The diary and drawings of Samuel Davis 1783.**
Michael Aris. London: Serindia, 1982. 124p. bibliog.

English scholarship on India and the East is well known throughout the world. Davis, a young lieutenant in the Bengal Army, was appointed by Warren Hastings to join Samuel Turner's mission to Bhutan and Tibet as a draughtsman and surveyor. The drawings made by Samuel Davis in Bhutan, and the journal he kept there, form the subject of this book. The volume covers religion, government, peasantry, medicine, architecture, buildings, festivals, food, and the climate of the country. There are many

drawings and plates reproducing objects and buildings of interest, and the whole work gives an excellent picture of Bhutan at that time.

111 **The cyclopaedia of India and of Eastern and Southern Asia, commercial, industrial, and scientific; products of the mineral, vegetable, and animal kingdoms, useful arts and manufactures.**
Edward Balfour. London: Bernard Quaritch, 1885. 3 vols.
Volume one contains (on pages 354-5) a brief article on the history, topography, and religion of Bhutan from 1772 to 1880. A bibliography of some important books on Bhutan is given at the end of the article.

112 **Anglo-Assamese relations 1771-1826.**
S. K. Bhuyan. Gauhati, India: Department of Historical and Antiquarian Studies, Government of Assam, 1949. 636p. bibliog.
Bhuyan describes the relations between Assam and the British East India Company between 1771 and 1826, using both English and local Assamese sources. Pages 34-6, 71-82, 314-19, 324-9, 376-7 and 502-5, provide an historical analysis of the Bhutan Duars, who inhabit the range of mountains separating southern Bhutan from Assam, and their relations with the British. Amongst the other subjects discussed are: relations of the British government with the hill tribes of Assam; trade competition between the British, Europeans and Indians; Captain Thomas Welsh's expedition into Assam; recrudescence of Burkendaze troubles (Burkendazes were the residents of North Gauhati who were revolting against the British); and the intricacies of the East India Company's Assam policy. This volume provides a thorough review of the importance of Assam and Bhutan to the British during this period.

113 **Bhutan and the British.**
Peter Collister. London: Serindia with Belitha Press, 1987. 210p.
This book provides an introduction to Bhutan through the writings of British travellers and the official correspondence of the British Government. It is a summary of the published reports of the successive British Government missions to Bhutan, from George Bogle's in 1774-75 to that of Ashley Eden in 1863-64. For the subsequent period until 1947, Collister's chief source was the unpublished official correspondence and annual reports of the Political Officers based in Sikkim and stored in the India Office Library and Records in London. Reading this work gives a clearer understanding of Bhutan's place with regard to the overall British policy in the Indian subcontinent. The book is illustrated with a number of black-and-white plates of oil paintings, aquatint and watercolours of the eighteenth century and 28 very interesting pictures of Bhutan taken between 1905 and 1907.

114 **Bhutan and India. A study in frontier political relations (1772-1865).**
Arabinda Deb. Calcutta: Firma KLM, 1976. 190p. map. bibliog.
This is a very good attempt to analyse Bhutan's history during this period. The book begins by describing the beautiful land, its people, and the system of government which at the time was different from those of most of the countries of the world. Officialdom in Bhutan was a mixture of lay and Lamaist elements. The Drukpa (the Tibetan Buddhist sect which had settled in Bhutan) had a creed that enjoined celibacy for its officials, but it was ignored by the powerful lay aristocracy. The study of the Bhutanese hierarchy and the system of administration, together with Bhutan's trade

relations with the British, are very interesting to read. The story of the British conquest of Assam and Bhutan, and an examination of Bhutan's land revenue administration, produce an analysis of the motives of British policy towards Bhutan during the Governorship of Dalhousie from 1848 to 1865.

115 **George Bogle's treaty with Bhutan (1775).**
     Arabinda Deb. *Bulletin of Tibetology*, vol. 8, no. 1 (1971), p. 5-14.
Arabinda gives a succinct view of George Bogle's commercial treaty with Bhutan in May 1775 with Deb Raja of Bhutan, a treaty which conceded important privileges to Bhutanese traders and complemented the Anglo-Bhutanese treaty of April 1774 which had ended the First Bhutan War. The author quotes the most significant provisions of the treaty ensuring 'the continuance of ancient trade with trans-Himalayas through native agencies, though perhaps on a diminished scale, for the next half century'. Bogle probed the political situation in Bhutan, locating the de facto sovereignty and prescribing British protocol for the following century. The author discusses the succeeding relationships and the efficacy of the contacts and policies established.

116 **A note concerning early Anglo-Bhutanese relations.**
     A. Field. *East and West*, vol. 13 (Dec. 1962), p. 340-5.
Field offers a straightforward account of the British period, focusing on political history of the country. The article is particularly useful to those who want to know the British attitude towards Bhutan up to George Bogle's mission to that country in 1774.

117 **Bayonets to Lhasa: the first full account of the British invasion of Tibet in 1904.**
     Peter Fleming. London: Rupert Hart-Davis, 1961. 319p. bibliog.
Fleming provides an account of the invasion of Tibet in 1904, together with a detailed narrative of events. While not radically revising the general picture given by earlier works, the author nonetheless fills in details, making considerable use of English sources. Pages 26-8, 141-2 and 199-200 provide descriptions of Bhutan and of its relations with India.

118 **Godwin Austen's map of western Bhutan and his survey report, 1864.**
     Indian Historical Records Commission Proceedings, vol. 31, no. 2 (Jan. 1955), p. 86-96.
In 1863, the British authorities sent a goodwill mission, headed by Ashley Eden, Chief Secretary to the Government of Bengal, and Captain Austen was engaged as a Surveyor and Deputy to Mr Eden. Captain Godwin Austen submitted his map and survey report to the Surveyor-General of India on 15 July 1864. The papers in this volume were originally read at the 31st meeting of the Commission held at Mysore, India on 2 January 1955, and this particular paper tries to establish what factors were responsible for the creation of Austen's map of western Bhutan and what it aimed to achieve. The map was meant to indicate the boundaries clearly, and also to discourage frequent raids in the Assam and Bengal Duars from the subordinate Bhutia officials who acted independently of the central control of the Bhutan government. The paper also contains some very interesting information on the government of the time; religion and the monastic system; agriculture; and the forts at Daling (Ambiokh), Paro, and Ponaka [Punakna].

119   **British relations with Bhutan.**
Shantiswarup Gupta.   Jaipur, India: Panchsheel Prakashan, 1974,
223p. 5 maps. bibliog.
This book forms part of the author's thesis submitted to Allahabad University in 1946,
and was published because of Bhutan's importance in the world. It covers the period
from 1772 to the end of the Second World War and examines topics such as the
internal conditions of Bhutan up to 1880; the first contact made with Bhutan; and the
political and commercial relations of the country. The appendixes include the
agreement signed by Mr Eden and the Bhutanese envoys.

120   **A statistical account of Bengal.**
W. W. Hunter.   London: Turner & Co., 1876. 20 vols.
William Wilson Turner was Director-General of Statistics to the Government of India
and these volumes are packed with information on Bengal. Volume 10 (pages 120-2)
provides information on the poll tax paid by the Bhutanis in lieu of land revenue in the
hilly tract called Dalingkot, annexed from Bhutan in 1865. Pages 218-23 deal with the
early history and a brief historical sketch of the relations between the Indian
Government and Bhutias, a relationship which ultimately led to the extension of the
British frontier in this direction.

121   **Himalayan triangle: a historical survey of British India's relations with
Tibet, Sikkim and Bhutan, 1765-1950.**
Amar Kaur Jasbir Singh.   London: British Library, 1988. 408p.
bibliog.
A very useful contribution to the British Indian history of these Himalayan kingdoms,
this volume is not only an historical survey which examines in detail the diplomatic
relationship between British India and the states of Tibet, Sikkim and Bhutan; it also
presents an integrated appraisal of the development of these three kingdoms with their
closely interlinked political and religious ties. On pages 291-380 it provides information
on the first contacts between Bhutan and the East India Company, 1766-92; Bhutan,
the Gurkhas and the Indo-Nepalese war, 1793-1816; the Assam Duars and Indo-
Bhutanese relations, 1825-38; Eden's, Macaulay's, and Charles Bell's missions to
Bhutan; Anglo-Bhutan war and demarcation of the Indo-Bhutan frontier, 1865-72;
British suzerainty in Bhutan and the Chinese claim to suzerainty in Bhutan, 1905-10;
Bhutan in treaty relations with the Crown, 1911-45; the end of the British connection
and the status of Bhutan, 1946-50.

122   **India and Bhutan: a study in interrelations 1772-1910.**
Manorama Kohli.   New Delhi: Munshiram Manoharlal, 1982. 240p.
bibliog.
This is a critical study of the relations between India and Bhutan at a period of time
during which the British colonial power in India was seeking to enlarge its hold on the
subcontinent. The author traces British policy with regard to Bhutan, a gradual process
developed under the pressure of circumstances. In narrating the evolution of the policy
Kohli has worked chronologically and historically since that method enables readers to
follow more easily the logical process of development. Within this broad historical
perspective, the facts and situations have been analysed critically and objectively from
the point of view of inter-state relations seen in the context of the British Indian policy
and with particular reference to the eastern Himalayan region.

123   **The Himalayan frontier during the British rule in India: a case study of the Bhutanese frontier.**
Kapileshwar Labh.   *Journal of Indian History*, vol. 61, no. 1-3 (1983), p. 185-96.

Labh has tried to analyse the evolution of British political ties with the Himalayan states, and in particular, with Bhutan. The author contends that the East India Company was determined to avoid deep political involvement in the Himalayan states, choosing instead to use them as buffers to Chinese interests, an attitude which influenced subsequent British policy. The limited economic opportunities further diminished large-scale British interests. The Chinese invasion of Tibet in 1910 did, however, elicit a strong British statement, opposing the possible intrusion of China's interests into the buffer areas.

124   **History of the relations of the government with the hill tribes of the North-East Frontier of Bengal.**
Sir Alexander Mackenzie.   Calcutta: Home Department Press, 1884. 582p.

This book is based on the official sources of the British Government and includes the history of the North-East Frontier, together with a sketch of British relations with Bhutan, the Bhutan war, and later events in Bhutan. It includes an account of trade between Assam and Tibet and there is also a description of various tribes inhabiting the area.

125   **The North-East Frontier of India.**
Sir Alexander Mackenzie, prefatory introduction to the new edition by B. K. Roy Burman.   Delhi: Mittal, 1989. 586p.

The North-East Frontier of Bengal embraces the whole of the hill ranges north, east, and south of the Assam Valley, as well as the western slopes of the great mountain system lying between Bengal and independent Burma, with its outlying spurs and ridges. On the subject of Bhutan (pages 9-19) Mackenzie traces the political relations of the Indian Government with Bhutan from 1828 to 1880. The topics covered are the British mode of dealing with the Bhutias, troubles on the India-Bhutan border, and the missions to Bhutan of Mr Pemberton in 1837 and Mr Eden in 1864. Sir Alexander Mackenzie was a government official and he compiled this account from the official records of the British India Government. The book was first published in 1884.

126   **History and culture of the Indian people.**
R. C. Majumdar.   Bombay: Bharatiya Vidya Bhavan, 1963. 11 vols.

Pages 671 and 1020-5 of volume ix – British paramountcy and Indian renaissance – present a detailed discussion of the history of Bhutan in the eighteenth and nineteenth centuries. The British-Bhutan treaty of 1865 is also mentioned.

127   **Narrative of the mission of George Bogle to Tibet, and of the journey of Thomas Manning to Lhasa.**
Clements Robert Markham.   London: Trubner, 1879. 362p. maps.

Bogle provided the first account of an English mission to Bhutan, but prior to this work no full account of Bogle's mission of 1774 had been published. This volumes provides early first-hand information on Bhutan, its inhabitants, and their history and religion. It is also clear from the text that Indo-Bhutanese trade was greatly increased by the reduction and abolition of duties on the frontier, and by establishing an annual fair at Rangpur which continued till 1832. The credit for the publication of this most useful book goes to C. R. Markham since the papers relating to Bogle's mission – sent to the Home Government by Warren Hastings in 1774 – were lost. In 1875, Markham, Secretary to Lord Northbrook, compiled a good account of George Bogle's mission to Bhutan from the journals, memoranda and correspondence preserved by his family in Scotland.

128 **National Day celebration at Paro.**
Kuensel News Bulletin, vol. 17, no. 51 (19 Dec. 1982), p. 1-4.

The sixth National Day of Bhutan was celebrated with great pomp and pageantry at Paro Dzongkhag on 17 December 1982. The King (HM Jigme Singye Wangchuck) gave a brief history of his dynasty from 1907 (when Ugyen Wangchuck became king) to the present day; he also pointed out that all the development activities in Bhutan for the last 21 years had been directed towards the welfare of the people and improving their economic conditions. He further added that the Bhutanese people should not be afraid of developments and informed them about the forthcoming developments in the Fifth Plan.

129 **Papers relating to Bootan; presented to Parliament by Her Majesty's Command.**
London: House of Commons, 15 Feb. 1865. 339p. map.

This volume brings together all of the official British government papers concerning Bhutan between 1855 and 1865. A large portion of the text is dominated by the events in 1864 which included Ashley Eden's mission to Bhutan. The papers have great historical value regarding Britain's relations with Bhutan; they also reveal its attitude towards Bhutan.

130 **Report on Bootan.**
R. Boileau Pemberton.   Calcutta: G. H. Huttmann, 1839. 212p. maps.

Captain Pemberton was an official envoy to Bhutan and his report contains his observations of Bhutan, its system of administration, its people, and both their social and religious customs. Besides containing a one-sided account of Anglo-Bhutanese relations over the Assam and Bengal Duars, it also gives a good account of Bhutan's rivers, roads, geology, government, priesthood, revenue, military resources, agricultural products, manufacturers, trade, population, and both its social and civil state.

131 **The first Bhutan mission to Ahom – court in 1801-1802.**
J. N. Phukan.   *Journal of Indian History*, vol. 59, no. 1-3 (1981), p. 225-33.

Phukan relates the developments surrounding the relations of Bhutan and Assam and the former's initial foreign mission to the Ahom capital. Ahom, a branch of the Tai family, gave their name to the people and province of Assam (India). From the available chronicles the author traces the daily progress of the Bhutan mission, the exchange of gifts, and the assurances of mutual good faith. The delegation's essential mission was to seek Assam's suppression of the bandits who were committing crimes on their mutual border.

132 **Political missions to Bhootan, comprising the reports of the Hon'ble Ashley Eden, 1864; Capt. R. B. Pemberton, 1837, 1838, with Dr. W. Griffiths's journal; and the account by Baboo Kishen Kant Bose.**
Calcutta: Printed at the Bengal Secretariat Office, 1865. 137, 206p. map.

These reports were written for the British India Government. Mr Ashley Eden's mission to Bhutan was the second one sent by the British Government. The mission, a failure, was one cause of the Duar war and the consequent annexation of the Duar territory from the Bhutanese by the British in India. These three reports and a journal provide background material on the history and culture of the people, and include coverage of such varied topics as geography, sociology, social customs, manufacture, wildlife, geology, botanical geography, the government of Bhutan and its military resources, and the priesthood.

133 **Bhutan between two worlds.**
Kamaljeet Rattan. *India Today*, vol. 14, no. 17 (1-15 Sept. 1989), p. 70-2.

This article provides an intimate view of modernization alongside of the traditional lifestyle in Bhutan. With the beginning of modern communications and trade and industry, the rich and middle-class Bhutanese people are trying to copy the Western lifestyle as they see it – by wearing jeans and playing golf. In order to achieve equilibrium between modernization and the traditional culture the King of Bhutan (Jigme Singye Wangchuck) launched 'Driglam Namza' which means a revival of Bhutanese traditional culture. The government is also trying to develop its official language called Dzongka (a sort of Tibetan). It has been made compulsory as a second language in all the English-medium schools. The modernization programme includes Bhutanese satellite television, free education and health, and modern cost-effective administration. Bhutan is one of the few nations who are trying to keep a balance between modernization and a traditional culture.

134 **Bhotan and the story of the Doar war.**
David Field Rennie. New Delhi: Manjuari, 1970. 408p. map. (Bibliotheca Himalayica series 1, vol. 5).

First published in London by John Murray in 1866, Dr Rennie's book gives a detailed sketch of the country, its inhabitants, and the form of government up to 1865. He refers to the commencement of British intercourse with Bhutan in 1772, and explains the situation in Bhutan up to 1815. An explanation is given of the annexation of Assam in 1828, and the first regular mission sent to Bhutan by the Government of India in 1837 is described. Rennie also mentions the second mission, headed by the Honourable Ashley Eden, which was a failure and was the immediate cause of the Doar/Duar war (so called from the name of the territory belonging to Bhutan). The origin and development of the Duar war is fully explained.

135 **An account of an embassy to the court of the Teshoo Lama in Tibet; containing a narrative of a journey through Bootan and part of Tibet. To which are added, views taken on the spot by Lieutenant Samuel Davis, and observations botanical, mineralogical and medical by Mr. Robert Saunders.**

Samuel Turner. London: Printed by W. Bulmer & Co., and sold by Messrs. G. & W. Nicol, Bookseller to His Majesty, 1800. 473p.

Captain Turner was employed by the East India Company, and his narrative of his visit to Bhutan forms an excellent picture of the country. At that time the country was divided into two rival camps, and he gives an eye-witness account of the 1783 civil war in Bhutan, which the Zimpon of Wandiphodrang had engineered. After witnessing the Zimpon's defeat by the King, Captain Turner describes his visits to the fortresses at Wangdiphodrang and Punakha. Turner's book is well illustrated with pencil drawings of Bhutan by Lieutenant Davis of the Bengal Engineer Corps, a noted artist who accompanied him.

136 **India's role in the emergence of contemporary Bhutan.**

Ravi Verma. Delhi: Capital, 1988. 290p. bibliog.

Verma has provided a comprehensive account of how free India, departing radically from the tradition of British India's role in Bhutan, has helped and promoted the emergence of that country as a sovereign state, from being a semi-soveriegn one, and as a modern state, from having been an extremely underdeveloped one. There are five chapters in the book. The first deals with Bhutan's history and its relations with British India; the second surveys India's vital contributions to Bhutan's economic and social development. The third chapter studies the country's general political development, democratization of its government, and modernization of its administrative machinery with India's help. Chapter four concerns India's assistance in the evolution of Bhutan's international personality and the expansion of its external relations, while the last chapter is a survey of the nature and extent of Bhutan's defence problems and India's willingness to help in the event of any danger from outside.

137 **Sikhim and Bhutan, twenty-one years on the North-East Frontier 1887-1908.**

J. Claude White. London: Edward Arnold, 1909. 331p. map.

The author provides an objective study using his intimate personal knowledge. He was an Indian civil servant who spent over thirty-two years of his active service in India, and of that, more than twenty years were spent in the administration of the North-East Frontier, Bhutan and Sikkim. The work is an extremely good account of these countries, both geographically and historically, as well as of the personal experiences of the author during his many tours there. He has also given a very full account of his missions and explorations in Bhutan.

138 **India and Tibet: a history of the relations which have subsisted between the two countries from the time of Warren Hastings to 1910; with a particular account of the mission to Lhasa of 1904 – with maps and illustrations.**
Sir Francis Younghusband.   London: John Murray, 1910. 455p.

This book is an account of British relations with Tibet, the mission to Lhasa of 1904 being merely the culmination of a long series of efforts to regularize a good and permanent relationship between India and Tibet in a business-like manner. On pages 4-32 Younghusband provides George Bogle's 'Account of Bhutan, 1774' (*see also* Markham, *Narrative of the mission of George Bogle . . .*), and Samuel Turner's 'Account of the Embassy to the court of the Teshoo Lama, 1800' (q.v.). These were the first two official reports on Bhutan, and they provide eye-witness accounts of the history, culture and religion, and of the civil war in Bhutan in 1783.

Minorities and Immigrants

139 **Bhutan Assembly postpones deportation of Tibetans.**
Tibetan Review, vol. 14, no. 12 (Dec. 1979), p. 20-1.
This article surveys the problem of Tibetan refugees in Bhutan. It is pointed out that the 4,000 refugees who are unwilling to accept Bhutanese citizenship should not be deported to Tibet, and more time should be given to find suitable homes for the unfortunate refugees. There was also hope at the time that the Dalai Lama would help in finding homes for these refugees in India.

140 **Bhutan problem nears solution.**
Tibetan Review, vol. 15, no. 11 (Nov. 1980), p. 5-6.
A brief report on Tibetan refugees in Bhutan who were not allowed to stay there on account of their refusal to accept Bhutanese citizenship, a problem which now seems to be approaching a solution. The relations between the 4,000 Tibetans in Bhutan and their host government have deteriorated continuously since March 1974 when a number of them were arrested on the charge of an attempted coup. India, Canada, and New Zealand are trying to help some of the refugees to settle in their countries.

141 **Bhutanese allegations – Tibetan denial.**
Tibetan Review, vol. 9, no. 5-6 (May-June 1974). p. 10-12.
Recently it was disclosed in the National Assembly of Bhutan that Mr Gyalo Thondrup, brother of the exiled Dalai Lama, and Mr Phintso Thonde, representative of the Dalai Lamai in Delhi, were plotting to assassinate the King, His Majesty Jigme Singye Wangchuck of Bhutan. The Tibetan refugees in India had denied the allegation. This article is a published version of the allegation, along with the denial and motives behind the sinister plot.

Minorities and Immigrants

142 Fate of Tibetans in Bhutan remains undecided.
Tibetan Review, vol. 14, no. 9 (Sept. 1979), p. 5-6.
This article examines a recent decision of the National Assembly of Bhutan to repatriate to Tibet 4,000 Tibetan refugees who are settled in Bhutan and are refusing to accept Bhutanese citizenship. Bhutan believes that the refugees are trying to create a Tibetan state within Bhutan as they are refusing to accept Bhutanese citizenship and are also paying taxes to the Tibetan administration at Dharmsala (India).

143 First batch of Tibetans from Bhutan coming out in March.
Tibetan Review, vol. 16, no. 2 (Feb. 1981), p. 5-7.
This report shows that the work of providing a new home for 3,000 Tibetans in Bhutan is progressing slowly. About 1,500 people are being allowed to settle in India and about three to four hundred of these Tibetans are also being allowed to settle in Canada and New Zealand. These Tibetans have been living in Bhutan ever since their escape from Tibet in 1959, and now they are being forced to leave Bhutan as they have refused to accept Bhutanese citizenship. About 1,000 Tibetans who have accepted Bhutanese citizenship will be allowed to continue to stay in Bhutan.

144 Tibetans in Bhutan: problem of repatriation.
R. C. Misra. *China Report*, vol. 18, no. 5, (1982), p. 25-32.
In 1959 Bhutan gave shelter to approximately 4,000 Tibetans fleeing their country, and tolerated them for 20 years until 1979 when they were asked to leave. Misra analyses the internal factors and the activities of the Tibetans which underlie the decision of expulsion, chief amongst which is the Tibetans' refusal to change their nationality and merge into their new surroundings.

145 Solving the refugee problem. Exiled Tibetans decide to become Bhutanese citizens after failing to find a home in India and getting a threat of deportation.
Mohan Ram. *Far Eastern Economic Review*, vol. 109 (11 July 1980), p. 32-3.
From 1911 to 1950, Tibet was virtually an independent country, but its status as such was never officially recognized by China. In October 1950, Chinese Communist forces invaded Tibet and in 1954 the Government of India recognized Tibet as an integrated part of China. Since 1950 Tibetan refugees have been living in Bhutan with the hope of returning back to a 'free' Tibet, but in May 1979, the Bhutan government decided to take a tough line and told the refugees either to become their citizens or prepare to be deported back to Tibet. The article discusses the problem of the refugees and how to integrate them into the national life of Bhutan in their new role as citizens.

146 Tibetans in Bhutan to be pulled out.
Tibetan Review, vol. 13, no. 11 (Nov. 1978), p. 7-8.
This is a report on the pitiable condition of Tibetans in Bhutan who have refused to accept Bhutanese citizenship. It highlights their present state of uncertainty and fear as they would have to leave their immovable property which they have built during the last 20 years in Bhutan. It is also suggested that these Tibetans should be allowed to settle in Arunachal Pradesh (India) so that some of them would be absorbed in the communal plots of land in some of the existing agricultural settlements, and thus the abruptness of change would not be so severe.

Languages

General

147 **The linguistic survey of India.**
Edited by Sir George Grierson.   Calcutta: Superintendent of
Government Printing, 1909. 11 vols.
The main Tibeto-Burman languages of Nepal (including Tibetan dialects) are treated
on pages 106-567 in volume three of this extremely useful work. The whole survey
covers the languages of India/South Asia, and the Nepali language is discussed in
volume nine, part four, on pages 1-99. The Nepali grammar and its specimen texts,
with Roman transliteration and English translation, are very useful for information on
the origins of the Nepali language. The work was reprinted in Delhi by Motilal
Barnarsidas in 1967.

148 **Nepali: a national language and its literature.**
Michael James Hutt.   New Delhi: Sterling; London: School of
Oriental and African Studies, 1988. 252p. bibliog. map.
The author, a lecturer on the Nepali language in the London University School of
Oriental and African Studies (SOAS), reveals the present status of Nepali in its
national and regional context, discusses its links with the development of Nepalese
nationalism, and examines progress towards standardization of grammar and spelling.
Most of the book is devoted to an examination of medieval and modern Nepali
literature.

149 **Basic course in spoken Nepali.**
Tika B. Karki, Chij K. Shrestha.   Kathmandu: Karki and Shrestha,
1985. 2nd ed. 266p. bibliog.
The course was designed to give speech and reading practice for self-instructional
purposes. In the 41 lessons, grammar is illustrated in dialogues and topically arranged
sentences, and explained in notes. The lessons are in Roman script only, but the

introductory section on pronunciation uses both Roman and Devanagari script in parallel. This is a very good book based on the materials developed for teaching Peace Corps Volunteers. It also includes a topical vocabulary list.

150   A course in Nepali.

David J. Matthews.   London: School of Oriental and African Studies; New Delhi: Heritage, 1984. 344p.

Dr Matthews is a Senior Lecturer at SOAS, University of London, and the textbook was based on materials used for teaching Nepali at that institution. After an introductory section on the Nepali script and its pronunciation, twenty lessons demonstrate all the principal structures of the language, explanations being followed by reading passages and sentences for translation from and into Nepali. Devanagari script is used throughout – except in the exercises. It is an extremely useful book for anyone learning Nepali.

151   The Tibetan system of writing.

Roy Andrew Miller.   Washington, DC: American Council of Learned Societies, 1956. 30p. (Program in Oriental Languages, Publications Series B-Aids-No. 6).

This short publication was designed to give reading practice. The phonemes, and the symbols used to represent them in the Tibetan script, are described in articulatory terms, with the aid of transcription. The basic principles of spelling are outlined both in transcription and in Tibetan script.

152   Manual of the Sikkim Bhutia language or Denjong-ke.

Graham Sandberg.   London: Constable, 1895. 2nd ed. 144p.

This manual was the first work on the Bhutia language in English. It includes grammar, an English–Denjong-ke dictionary, a list of Lepcha words and phrases, and exercises in colloquial phrases. Bhotia/Bhutia is a general name given to the group of dialects of the Tibeto-Chinese family of languages which are spoken by the people all along the Indo-Tibetan border. Bhotia is also used as another name for the Bhutani of Bhutan.

153   A Nepali conversational manual.

Ruth Laila Schmidt.   Philadelphia, Pennsylvania: University of Pennsylvania, 1968. 139p.

This work was designed to give speech and reading practice on a self-instructional basis. In the 27 lessons, dialogues and narratives serve as a base for structured conversation. Grammar is explained in structural terms. There are response, transformation, and substitution drills. A vocabulary list is given for each lesson. Even though it is an old publication, it still is a very useful one.

154   The National Library of Bhutan: preserving the nation's heritage.

Felicity M. Shaw.   *HKLA Journal (Hong Kong)*, vol. 9 (1985), p. 39-58.

The author, who is a Law Librarian from the University of Hong Kong, visited Bhutan and wrote this article on the history and collection of the National Library. The Library was established in 1969, and its aim was to collect and preserve both ancient and modern works from Bhutan and Tibet, relating to religion, culture, history, and traditions. The Library is in Thimphu, the capital of Bhutan. The National Library Book-store opened in 1980 and is also housed in the National Library building. The Library stock consists of about 400 books in English, 50 periodical titles in English and the rest of the 10,000 books are in Tibetan. The National Library sells its publications through the National Library Book-store in Thimphu.

155 **Origin and development of the Nepali language.**
Dayanand Shrivastava, foreword by Sukumar Sen. Calcutta: Calcutta University Press, 1962. 145p.

The author traces the development of the sounds and grammatical forms of Nepali and also discusses the relationship of the language to the rest of the Indo-Aryan group. The book is useful mainly to the linguist.

156 **Glottal stop and glottal constriction in Lepcha.**
R. K. Sprigg. *Bulletin of Tibetology*, vol. 3, no. 1 (Feb. 1966), p. 5-15.

The Lepcha are a Mongolian tribe forming a large part of the population of Sikkim, Bhutan and Darjeeling. The author, a well-known philologist, now retired from being Reader in Tibeto-Burman languages at the School of Oriental and African Studies, University of London, wrote this highly technical article after visiting Nepal, Sikkim and Tibet. Sprigg concludes that Lepcha makes considerable use of both glottal closure and glottal constriction. Both features may be used stylistically, to bring a word into prominence within the sentence; and for such words these features are alternative features only. This alternation of glottal closure and glottal constriction with the absence of these features is purely Lepcha, and has nothing to do with Tibetan.

Dictionaries

157 **English–Tibetan colloquial dictionary.**
Charles A. Bell. Alipore, India: West Bengal Government Press, 1965. 2nd ed. 562p.

This is basically a word list, with parts of speech occasionally listed. It also introduces the important rules of writing and reading Tibetan.

158 **Tibetan–English dictionary with supplement.**
Stewart H. Buck. Washington, DC: Catholic University of America Press, 1969. 833p.

The entries in this dictionary include grammatical information, common synonyms and illustrative phrases. The author gives special attention to the technical vocabularies of Buddhism, mythology, and astrology, and he also includes a brief sketch of the Tibetan language and a history of Tibetan lexicography.

159 **Angreji–Nepali sajha samkshipta shabdakosh.** (Sajha concise
English–Nepali dictionary.)
Narendra Mani Dixit.   Kathmandu: Sajha, 1987. 2nd ed.
The author, a great scholar and a prominent civil servant, spent about 50 years in
compiling this dictionary. There are about 26,000 main entries, and many technical
words are included in it. This is the best English–Nepal dictionary available in print.

160 **An English–Tibetan dictionary; containing a vocabulary of
approximately twenty thousand words with their Tibetan equivalents.**
Compiled by Kazi Dawa Sam Dup.   New Delhi: Oriental Books
Reprint Corporation, distributed by Munshiram Manoharlal Publishers
(Delhi), 1973. 2nd ed. 989p.
This is a very useful dictionary for advanced-level students as well as for ordinary
people learning Tibetan.

161 **A comparative dictionary of the languages of India and High Asia; with
a dissertation based on the Hodgson lists, official records and
manuscripts.**
William Wilson Hunter.   London: Trubner, 1868. 218p.
The author was a Fellow of the Ethnological Society of Her Majesty's Bengal Civil
Service. The book is one of the first philological investigations and compilations. Part 1
is devoted to remarks about the politics and languages of India and her frontier
regions. The body of the work consists of a comparative listing of words: at the head of
each page, a word is given in its French, German, English, Russian, and Latin forms;
the same word is then listed in some 142 dialects from the geographical area of India
and High Asia. This includes all the dialects of the Himalayan region.

162 **A Tibetan–English dictionary, with special reference to the prevailing
dialects. To which is added an English–Tibetan vocabulary.**
Heinrich A. Jäschke.   London: Routledge & Kegan Paul, 1975. 671p.
This is a very useful and comprehensive dictionary, in which the entries are also given
in Roman characters. The book was first published in London in 1882.

163 **English–Nepali dictionary.**
Robert Kilgour, revised and arranged by H. C. Duncan.   Darjeeling,
India: Government Branch Press, 1923. 391p.
This dictionary has approximately 13,500 entries. The Nepali material is in both the
Nepali and the Roman script. It is still a popular dictionary with people who have little
knowledge of Nepali script.

164 Dictionary of the Lepcha language.
George Byres Mainwaring, revised and completed by Albert
Grünwedel. Berlin: Unger, 1898. 552p.

This is the most complete Lepcha–English dictionary in existence. According to the Linguistic Survey of India, Lepcha belongs to the Himalayan group of the Tibeto-Burman sub-family, and has some influence on Nepali, Bhotia and Tibeto-Chinese. Lepcha speakers are mostly bilingual.

165 New standard dictionary: English–Nepali.
Paras Mani Pradhan, Nagendra Mani Pradhan. Kalimpong, India:
Bhagyalaxmi, 1988. 3rd ed. 830p.

The dictionary contains about 29,000 entries, with pronunciation and parts of speech indicated. Appendices list words and phrases from other languages commonly used in English. It is primarily intended for use by Nepali students, and foreign learners of Nepali will need to use a Nepali–English dictionary in conjunction with this work in order to tell which of several Nepali equivalents is appropriate for a particular context.

166 Dictionary of the Bhotanta, or Boutan language; printed from a manuscript copy edited by John Marshman, to which is prefixed a grammar of the Bhotanta language, by W. Carey.
The Revd Frederic Christian Gotthelf Schroeter. Serampore, India:
Mission Press, 1826. 36, 475p.

The work consists of a grammar as well as a dictionary of the Bhotanta language of Tibet and Bhutan. The dictionary was written in Italian by some Roman Catholic missionaries, and has been partly translated into English by Mr Marshman.

Grammars

167 A colloquial grammar of the Bhutanese language.
Quintin Byrne. Allahabad, India: Pioneer Press, 1909. 72p.

The author has made a good attempt at describing the phonology, etymology and syntax of the language spoken by the Bhutanese people. A major portion of the book consists of vocabulary, conversation and phrases, and reading exercises.

168 Modern literary Tibetan: a grammar and reader.
Melvyn C. Goldstein, Tsering Dorje Kashi. Urbana, Illinois:
University of Illinois, Center for Asian Studies, 1973. 352p.
(Wolfenden Society on Tibeto–Burman Linguistics. Occasional Papers Series, Vol. 5).

This book may be used for self-instructional purposes. Part I is on Tibetan grammar; it is explained in structural terms, and is illustrated in basic sentences and graded readings. Part II consists of readings in modern Tibetan. These readings are selected from Tibetan, Bhutanese, Sikkimese and Chinese published materials. Part III contains a glossary and a morphological index.

169 **Tibetan word-book.**
Basil John Gould, Hugh Edward Richardson.   London: Oxford
University Press, 1943. 447p.

This book is intended for people who are intending to learn Tibetan. It is arranged in
Tibetan alphabetical order, and each syllable is given a key number. In the first line of
the entry, syllables are dealt with singly; the arrangement is key number, phonetic
rendering, the syllable in Tibetan characters, a letter-by-letter transcription of the
Tibetan character, and a catch meaning. In the subsequent line the arrangement is the
word or phrase in Tibetan characters, the key numbers of the syllables in the word or
phrase, the meaning in English, and a phonetic rendering of the word or phrase.

170 **Grammar of the Tibetan language, literary and colloquial; with copious
illustrations, and treating fully of spelling, pronunciation, and the
construction of the verb, and including appendices of the various forms
of the verb.**
Herbert B. Hannah.   Delhi: Cosmo, 1973. 396p.

The book was first published in 1912. It is in three parts: Part I, phonology, the
spelling system and the parts of speech; Part II, functions of the parts of speech; and
Part III which deals briefly with syntax and has appendices on conjugation.

171 **First Bhutanese grammar.**
The Revd Ralph W. Hofrenning.   Chicago: Ebenezer Lutheran
Church, 1959. 13p.

The author claims that this is the first-ever attempt at writing a grammar in Gongor, an
unwritten language spoken in the eastern side of Bhutan – extending from Parkijuli
Mission, up into the hills of Bhutan. A number of languages and dialects are spoken in
Bhutan, and this is one of the major languages.

172 **Tibetan grammar. Supplement of readings with vocabulary, by John L.
Mish.**
Heinrich A. Jäschke.   New York: Frederick Ungar, 1954. 126p.

The book deals with phonology, etymology (morphology), and syntax. Tibetan–
English vocabulary is arranged according to the Tibetan alphabet. The appendix
includes a collection of phrases from daily life.

173 **A grammar of the Lepcha language.**
George Byres Mainwaring.   New Delhi: Manjusri, 1971. 146p.
(Bibliotheca Himalayica, series 2, vol. 5).

This is a reprint of the 1876 edition and provides one of the first grammatical studies on
the subject. It was primarily intended for the Lepcha speakers of the Himalayas. Part I
deals with the alphabet; Part II with monosyllables and disyllables; and Parts III and
IV with parts of speech and syntax. Appendices cover figurative and honorific
language, animal and child language, prosody, and the division of time. Rong script is
used throughout, with Roman transcription.

174 **Textbook of colloquial Tibetan: dialect of central Tibet.**

George N. Roerich, Lobsang Phuntshok Lhalungpa.   New Delhi: Manjusri, 1972. 2nd ed. 280p.

The book is designed to give speech and reading practice in three parts. Part I, grammar in traditional style; Part II, conversational exercises and topical conversational exercises; Part III contains Tibetan–English vocabulary. Appendices include the various styles of Tibetan writing, and a list of newly coined Tibetan political terms.

175 **Some Tsangla–Bhutanese sentences.**

E. Stack.   Shillong, India: Assam Secretariat Printing Press, 1897. 91p.

These sentences were designed to form Part III of a Tsangla–Bhutanese grammar, one of the many subjects connected with the languages and ethnography of the country on which the late Mr Stack was working. The other parts of the book were never published because of his untimely death. The text is in English.

Religion

176 **'The boneless tongue': alternative voice from Bhutan in the context of Lamaist societies.**
Michael Aris. *Past and Present*, vol. 115 (1987), p. 131-64.
Aris discusses unnoticed popular literature in Bhutan, which developed out of conflicts between the power of the institutional religion with its state trappings and the value of aspirations of the wider lay community. The work affords unique insight into common attitudes hidden between the visible superstructure of Lamaist societies of past and present. The texts stand as evidence for a cultural transition in Bhutan from a society dominated by monastic forms to one in which the value of the laity could find full expression. Inherently unstable, all theocracies associated with Lamaism collapsed because they could not deal effectively with internal feuding and the onslaught of modern ideologies. Bhutan is the only one to survive in modern times as an independent country. It appears to have done this by achieving its own transition from a weak theocracy to a powerful monarchy able to cope with the challenges of the 20th century.

177 **The religion of Tibet.**
Charles Alfred Bell. Oxford: Clarendon Press, 1931. 235p.
The title of the book is self-explanatory. The material for the work was gathered from books and manuscripts given to the author by the Dalai Lama and some leading Tibetans in Lhasa. Pages 53, 85, 124-6, and 213-16 cover Bhutan's own sect of Buddhism. There is also a discussion on the history of Bhutan, entitled 'The religious history of the south' (Tibetan title: 'Lho-i Cha-jung'). This book was given to the author by the late King of Bhutan.

178 **Buddhism: its essence and development.**
Edward Conze. Oxford: Bruno Cassirer, 1953. 2nd ed. 212p.
Anyone interested in a very popular, useful, comprehensive and at the same time easy-to-read account of Buddhism should read this book. Conze also provides information on early history, the monastic system, and Mahayana and Tantric Buddhism, making it

an extremely useful book for Western readers. A paperback edition was also published by Harper of New York in 1959.

179   **The Jataka or stories of the Buddha's former births.**
Edited by Edward B. Cowell.   Cambridge: Cambridge University Press, 1895-1913. 7 vols.
This is a collection of over five hundred tales of Buddha's former births, translated by various scholars. In Mahayana Buddhism, Buddha is described in the Jataka account by his former lives as the Bodhisattva (Buddhas of compassion), as love in action guided by wisdom. Jatakas are largely folk literature, in which beast fables, fragments of historical tradition, and the tales of wisdom have been gathered together with a religious and moral purpose. The value of the tales is that they form the basis and background of primitive Buddhism. Jatakas are thought-provoking, and I am sure the stories are very useful and will be read with profit and pleasure by everyone interested in Buddhism.

180   **An introduction to tantric Buddhism.**
Shahsi Bhushan Dasgupta.   Berkeley, California: Shambhala, 1974. 211p. bibliog.
In the eighth century AD Guru Padma Sambhava introduced the Mahayana school of Buddhism into Tibet, Bhutan, Sikkim and Nepal. The elements of tantricism which it includes are often described as a mixture of Shiva worship and magic. It lays emphasis on yogic practices and incantations addressed to the female Shaktis from whom human beings gain miraculous power. Dasgupta provides information on Buddhist tantras and the philosophical fragments found in them; different schools of tantric Buddhists; the elements of esoteric yoga; and the argument of the tantric Buddhists in defence of their yoga. The book was originally published in 1958 by Calcutta University Press.

181   **Ravaged treasures of the past – preservation of cultural heritage.**
Rigzin Dorji.   *Asian Culture*, vol. 35 (Summer/Autumn 1983), p. 40-6.
Although it contains some information on the history and civilization of Bhutan, this is principally an account of Buddhist temples and their architecture, literary language, historical records, religious order and the religious/cultural organizations of that country. It includes some discussion on the four major natural calamities (fire, water, earthquake and insects) against which the Royal Government of Bhutan has been fighting. The article is clearly written and is of interest to the general reader as well as to the specialist.

182   **Aspects of Mahayana Buddhism and its relation to Hinayana.**
Nalinaksha Dutt.   London: Luzac, 1930. 358p.
Mahayana Buddhism came to Bhutan in the eighth century AD. The object of this work is to present an exposition of the principal doctrines of Mahayana as found in the early Mahayanic treatises and to show the points of agreement and difference between the doctrines of Hinayana and Mahayana. It is an excellent review and comparative study of these two great schools of Buddhism.

Religion

183 Early monastic Buddhism.
Nalinaksha Dutt. Calcutta: Calcutta Oriental Press, 1941. 2 vols. 340, 349p. (Calcutta Oriental Series no. 30).

In the first volume the author has tried to answer three principal questions: what is not Buddhism, what is early (monastic) Buddhism, and how a Buddhist should live. The second volume contains three Buddhist Councils which are the three landmarks in the history and development of early monastic Buddhism. It also includes the history and literature of the Buddhist Schools of Thoughts and the doctrines of Group 1–5 Schools. The second volume ends with an analysis of the popular features which the religion incorporated in the pre-Ashokan and post-Ashokan periods, thus paving the way for the advent of Mahayana Buddhism. For the convenience of the general reader not acquainted with the phraseology of the Buddhist text, an exhaustive index of difficult words with their nearest English rendering has been added to the second volume. There is also a general index to both volumes.

184 Buddhist monks and monasteries of India: their history and their contribution to Indian culture.
Sukumar Dutt. London: George Allen and Unwin, 1962. 397p.

This book is very useful to anyone who wants to know about the ancient Buddhist past, for it is the first comprehensive account to be written on Buddhist Sangha – the monastic order which was founded by the Buddha, and whose members are called Bhikhus. It is the oldest monastic order in the world, and this book presents a good picture of its growth and development during the first three or four centuries of Buddhism.

185 Early Buddhist monachism 600 B.C.–100 B.C.
Sukumar Dutt. London: Kegan Paul, 1924. 196p.

Dutt offers a detailed history of Buddhist monks in this book which won the 1919 Griffith Memorial Prize in India for the most original research. The book includes: the laws of the Vinayapitaka and their interpretation; the primitive Paribrajakas – a theory of their origin; the Sangha and the development of Patimokkha; and the internal polity of a Buddhist Sangha (monk). It is one of the best books on the subject.

186 Studies in Bhutanese history dealing with the structural organisation of the Bhutanese theocracy.
Kathleen Frey. *Tibetan Review*, vol. 18, no. 4 (April 1983), p. 15-22.

Bhutan is unique, the first Buddhist theocracy established in history, and pre-dating the Tibetan theocracy by more than a century. Bhutan was originally divided into three areas by Ngwang Namgyal – West, East and South. Each of these areas was under the command of a monk (officially called Chila). This office was later changed to that of Penlop or Governor by the middle of the nineteenth century. The areas under the jurisdiction of the Penlops were divided into Dzongs, and the administrative centre of each Dzong was also called a Dzong. It is an important article for readers who wish to know about the history and structure of the Bhutanese theocracy, the genealogy of Ngwang Namgyal (1594-1691), and the structure of the theocracy from the Sovereign to the village headman.

187   **On the threshold of three closed lands: the guild outpost in the Eastern Himalayas.**
   J. A. Graham.   Edinburgh: Clark, 1897. 166p.

There are many references to Bhutan in this work about the Mission in Kalimpong, a mission which was maintained by the Church of Scotland Guilds for work in Tibet, Nepal and Bhutan. Buddhism and Lamaism are described in detail for the general reader.

188   **In the footsteps of the Buddha.**
   René Grousset, translated from French by J. A. Underwood.   New York: Grossman, 1971. 337p.

The author presents the history, legends and metaphysics of mediaeval Buddhism from the accounts of Chinese pilgrims in the 7th century AD. It also describes many different aspects of mediaeval Buddhism in India and China. Much material from modern scholarship and archaeological research is brought in as background and thus we learn as much about history as we do about religion and art.

189   **Guru Rinpoche.**
   Kuensel, vol. 20, no. 26 (30 June 1985), p. 2-4.

Discusses the life and teachings of Guru Rinpoche or, as he is usually known, Guru Rimpoche. His original name was Padma Sambhava, a native of northern India, who established Lamaism in Bhutan and Tibet about 747 AD. He belonged to the ritualistic and mystical Yogacharya sect and went to Tibet at the invitation of Khri Srong, the then King of Tibet. According to Tibetan Chronicles, Padma Sambhava resided in Tibet for about fifty years and announced his approaching departure from this world in 802 AD. In Bhutan he is highly regarded as the greatest saint who spread Mahayana Buddhism in the country. The article also discusses many festivals which are associated with the Guru.

190   **The monasteries of the Himalayas: Tibet, Bhutan, Ladakh, Sikkim.**
   Suzanne Held, foreword by Jean Chalon, introduction by Gérard Barrière, captions by Lise Medini, Gérard Barrière and translated by D. B. Tubbs.   Italy: Edita, 1988. 150p.

Suzanne Held, a professional photographer, has been travelling to Bhutan, Ladakh and Tibet for the last twelve years. She goes as a solitary pioneer and tries to capture the spirit of the region. This book, which contains a foreword, an introduction and 147 coloured photographs with captions, is divided into four chapters: On the path of the Gods; Magic of God and demons; Everyday gestures and rites; and Sacred masks and dances.

191   **Buddhist logic and epistemology: studies in the Buddhist analysis of inference and language.**
   Edited by Bimal Krishna Matilal, Robert D. Evans.   Dordrecht, The Netherlands; Boston, Massachusetts; Lancaster, England; Tokyo: D. Reidal, 1986, 303p. bibliog.

There are seventeen chapters in this book by seventeen different scholars from India, UK, Europe, Canada and USA. Among them, they provide an in-depth study of Buddhist logical theory, set against a background of Buddhist epistemology. Each author has used original texts (Sanskrit or Tibetan) for resolving logical issues and philosophical questions. Most of the essays were part of a seminar held at Oxford University in August 1982, under the auspices of the International Association of Buddhist Studies.

192 An introduction to Mahayana Buddhism with especial reference to Chinese and Japanese phrases.
William Montgomery Mcgovern.   London: Kegan Paul; New York: E. P. Dutton, 1922. 233p.

Buddhism is divided into two great schools, Mahayana and Hinayana. Both systems originated in India. The Mahayana adopted Sanskrit as its language and spread to Mongolia, China, Japan, Tibet, Bhutan, Sikkim and Nepal, and the Hinayana spread almost exclusively to Sri Lanka, Burma and Siam. The Mahayana evolved a mythology and mysticism of its own and advocates the recognition of various Buddhas of the past, present and the future – the Bodhisattvas, the theoretical divine Buddhas who see successive rebirth for the well-being of the human race. The book provides information on the evolution of Buddhism; the nature of the absolute and its relation to the universe; the doctrine of trinity; the Wheel of Life and the road to Nirvana; and a short history of Buddhism, together with principal Buddhist sects. The author, who was a lecturer in the School of Oriental and African Studies, University of London, provides here a very clear understanding of Mahayana Buddhism.

193 Ancient Bhutan: a study on early Buddhism in the Himalayas.
Blanche C. Olschak.   Zurich: Swiss Foundation for Alpine Research, 1979. 222p. map. bibliog.

In Bhutan the Mahayana Buddhist or Lamaist religion still continues from ancient times, but the Lamaist religion of Tibet is fast vanishing. Olschak gives a comprehensive picture of the ancient institutions and religion of the country, and also provides very useful information on Bhutan's social institutions from the first propagation of Buddhism (when three temples were built in Bhutan during the middle of the 7th century) up to the present time. The text is supported by illustrations.

194 Index of half verses in Pramanavartikabhasya.
Rupendra Kumar Pagariya.   Ahmedabad, India: Bharatiya Sanskrit Vidyamandir, 1970. 76p.

Pramanavartikabhasya is a philosophical work by a Buddhist Prajnakargupta of the 8th century AD, containing about 2,666 verses. The index was intended as an aid to research scholars engaged in critically editing the philosophical texts in order to fix the chronological order of Sanskrit writers.

195 Mahayana texts translated into western languages: a bibliographical guide.
Compiled by Peter Pfandt.   Cologne, West Germany: E. J. Brill, 1983. 167p.

Mahayana Buddhism is practised in Tibet, Bhutan and other Himalayan states. The teaching of Mahayana is more distinctly religious, making its appeal to the heart and not the mind, to the intuition rather than the intellect. This is a useful bibliography for people who cannot read the original texts in Tibetan, Sanskrit, Chinese and Japanese.

The book is alphabetically arranged according to the title, and has Sanskrit, Tibetan, Chinese and Japanese titles indexes.

196　**The heritage of the bhikhu: a short history of the bhikhu in educational, cultural, social and political life.**
Walpola Rahula, translated by K. P. G. Wijayasurendra, revised by the author.　New York: Grove, 1974. 176p. bibliog.

This book was first published in 1946, by a Buddhist monk who was deeply involved in the controversy that arose in the 1940s over the role of Buddhist monks in public affairs. The work is valuable for its perceptions of the Buddhist monks who were to be increasingly attracted into political activism. It also considers the developments from 1946 to 1973.

197　**Buddhism in Sikkim, Ladakh and Bhutan.**
C. Swaramamurti.　*The Light of Buddha*, V (1960), p. 34-8.

The author is a Keeper in the National Museum of India. He gives a general description on the organization, rites, chief monasteries, and the art of Lamaism in Bhutan, Ladakh and Sikkim.

198　**Tantra in Tibet: the great exposition of secret mantra.**
Tsong-Ka-Pa, translated and edited by Jeffrey Hopkins.　London: George Allen & Unwin, 1977. 252p. (The Wisdom of Tibet Series).

Tantra covers a vast number of forms for developing the innate psychic powers, and for producing magical effects by spells, mantras (hymns), and ceremonies of various kinds. It may be 'white' or 'black', according to the motives of the performer, and according to the methods used. Suffice it to say that the 'white' aspect deals with pure occultism: self-development by Raja Yoga; while the 'black' aspect is concerned with the worship of the female energy in nature. The author (Tsong-Ka-Pa, 1357-1419), founder of the Gelukpa order of Tibetan Buddhism, presents the main features of the whole Buddhist tantra system as well as the difference between sutra (Buddhist sacred literature) and tantra, the two divisions of Buddha's word. Mahayana Buddhism includes tantras, and its geographical area covers the countries of Tibet, Mongolia, Sikkim, Bhutan, China, Japan, Korea and Hawaii.

199　**Dictionary of early Buddhist monastic terms.**
C. S. Upasak.　Varanasi, India: Bharati Prakashan, 1975. 246p.

This work, which is based on original sources, contains about 2,000 terms of the Buddhist ecclesiastical order. Quotations are given to illustrate the meaning. It is a pioneer work, and more of an encyclopaedia than a dictionary.

200　**Mahāyāna Buddhism: the doctrinal foundations.**
Paul Williams.　London; New York: Routledge, 1989. 317p. bibliog.

Paul Williams is a practising Buddhist and a lecturer in Indo-Tibetan studies at the University of Bristol. He provides an accurate account of the principles of Mahayana Buddhism, and places Buddhist doctrine within a historical and cultural context, providing a basis for students to carry out further studies into Buddhist theory and practice. The book is intended for undergraduates as an introduction to the ideas of Mahayana Buddhism.

Religion

201 **The life and liberation of Padmasambhava: Padma bKa'i Thang.**
Recorded by Yeshe Tsogyal, rediscovered by Terchen Urgyan Lingpa,
translated into French as *Le Dict de Padma* by Gustave-Charles
Toussaint, translated into English by Kenneth Douglas and Gwendolyn
Bays, corrected with the original Tibetan manuscripts, and with an
introduction by Tarthang Tulku. Emeryville, California: Dharma,
1978, 2 vols.

This is a detailed biography with teachings of Padma Sambhava. He is known as the
'Lotus Born', a native of northern India, who established Lamaism in Tibet. He
belonged to the ritualistic and mystical Yogacharya sect founded by Aryasangha, and
went to Tibet in 747 AD from Nalanda University (India) at the invitation of Khri
Srong, the then King of Tibet. His influence has been considerable in the Himalayan
region. All the Himalayan sects of Buddhism claim Padma Sambhava as their founder.
He also contributed enormously to the diffusion of Tantric Buddhism in the Himalayan
region including Tibet, Nepal and Bhutan, around 800 AD, and he is the founder of the
Nyingmapa, an old school of Lamaism which still has numerous followers in Bhutan.

Society and Social Conditions

202 Between Sikkim and Bhutan: the Lepchas and Bhutias of Pedong.
Indira Awasthy.   Delhi: B. R. Publishing, 1978. 128p.

Awasthy wrote this book during her stay in Pedong from January to October 1977. Pedong is in the Chumbi Valley, situated at a distance of about 35 miles south of Gangtok (Sikkim), and about 12 miles north-east of Kalimpong. It was acquired by the British from Bhutan in 1964. The author provides information about the legends, customs, religion and history, and about the position of women and the condition of the people of Pedong in the late 1970s. The residents of Pedong consist of Lepchas, Bhutias and Nepalese.

203 The people of Tibet.
Charles Alfred Bell.   Oxford: Clarendon Press, 1928. 319p. bibliog.

Sir Charles Bell has made a very good attempt at describing the domestic life of the Tibetan people. On pages 32-4, 43-50, 55-63, 141-8, 218-19 and 292-3 the book includes the history of Bhutan, its crops and fruits, funeral rites, the laws against adultery, marriage laws, and many other varied topics such as: meat eating, slavery, tea drinking, the lawlessness of the Bhutanese, times for sowing and reaping the crops, Chumbi Valley grazing grounds, the peasant's life, and why cigarette smoking was prohibited.

204 Descriptive ethnology of Bengal.
Edward Tuite Dalton.   Calcutta: Superintendent of Government Printing, 1872. 327p.

Some useful information on the Akas or Arkas is given on pages 37-8 of this book. They are the only remaining occupants of the segment of hill country lying between the Dophla territory and Bhutan. Dalton includes information on their history, relations with the British government, their religion and the type of houses they live in. More information on Bhutan is scattered throughout the book, but there is a helpful index. The book is illustrated with lithographic portraits copied from photographs.

Society and Social Conditions

205 Lepcha, my vanishing tribe.
A. R. Foning.   Delhi: Sterling, 1987. 314p.

Dr Foning, himself from a Lepcha tribe, claims that he has presented in this book an inside view of the tribal population of Lepchas, their religious beliefs, social practices, and political institutions from ancient times. The original habitat of the Lepchas, described in their myths, was 'Mayel Lyang', and this territory is now part of Sikkim, Nepal and Bhutan. Pages 6-16, 18-19, 83-4, 134-8, 268-9, 277-85 and 303-4 together provide information about the clan's Bhutanese connections; class system, government and administration; kingship and the worship of upright stones (in invoking gods, appeasing devils and demons); and their ancient weapons which are still preserved in Bhutan. The details of parallels between Lepcha and Tibetan Buddhism as practised in Bhutan and Sikkim represent a valuable addition to knowledge of their religious beliefs.

206 On the aborigines of the sub-Himalayas.
Brian H. Hodgson.   *Journal of the Asiatic Society of Bengal*, vol. 16 (1847), p. 1235-46.

Hodgson provides a wide variety of facts about the people and the Himalayan region. This article provided one basis for W. W. Hunter's study *A comparative dictionary of the languages of India and High Asia* (q.v.).

207 Peoples of South Asia.
Clarence Maloney.   New York: Holt, Rinehart and Winston, 1974. 584p. bibliog.

This volume aims to present as complete an anthropology as possible of the South Asian subcontinent. It is intended for college students. On the subject of Bhutan (pages 398-9, 411-13) it includes information on prehistory, modern history, and the culture and language of the people viewed from an anthropological perspective.

208 Graham of Kalimpong.
James R. Minto.   Edinburgh: William Blackwood, 1974. 202p.

This is a biography of Dr John Anderson Graham, a missionary from Scotland, who was later known as Graham of Kalimpong (a hilly tract in the Darjeeling District of West Bengal). The title was given to him because of his missionary activities, during the course of which he built a church and hospital for the local people. His relations with Mahatma Gandhi, Jawaharlal Nehru and Rabindra Nath Tagore are also mentioned. On pages 165-90, the author describes Graham's visit to Bhutan and his influence on the Royal family and politics of Bhutan, and his efforts towards the development of Bhutan.

209 Bhutan: a land of transition.
B. C. Nag.   *Indo Asian Culture*, vol. 20, no. 1 (1971), p. 30-5.

The author surveys Bhutan's modernization programme in the 1970s. Bhutan applied for admission to the United Nations with Indian assistance. The King (Jigme Singye Wangchuck) has weakened the monarchical system of Bhutan and strengthened the popular assembly. Nag also considers the construction of roads and schools and the creation of a modern army with the help of India. He concludes that Bhutan is wide open to Chinese invasion from Tibet and that Indian assistance could reach the tiny kingdom only with considerable difficulty.

210   **A report on ethnographical research in the Sikkim Himalayas, 1950-53.**
René von Nebesky-Wojkowitz.   *Wiener völkerkundliche Mitteillungen*, vol. II, no. 1 (1954), p. 33-8.

The author describes the nature of his research on early Tibetan religious beliefs and their relations to the beliefs of some of the hill tribes, especially the Lepchas. The Lepchas are a Mongolian tribe who form a large part of the population of Sikkim, Darjeeling and Bhutan.

211   **Bhotia tribals of India: dynamics of economic transformation.**
R. R. Prasad.   New Delhi: Gian, 1989. 207p.

Bhotia is a generic term used to designate several socially unrelated groups in the Indo-Tibetan borderland of the Himalayan and trans-Himalayan regions. In the eastern Himalayas it includes people living in the Nepalese-Tibetan border areas, Tibetans living in Darjeeling and the inhabitants of Bhutan. Traditionally Bhotias were connected with trade and from time immemorial they traded between India and Tibet. The book covers only the Bhotias of Johar Valley, but in studying the adaptive processes of the Johari Bhotias, the other Bhotia groups (such as Jad, Tolcha, Marcha and Shauka) have been touched upon for the sake of comparison. The present study traces the history of their trading activities with Tibet from the beginning, and also their socio-cultural life. Due to the sudden disruption of trade with Tibet, the Bhotias were forced to seek an alternative source of livelihood which affected their pattern of life. The study, which covers a vast period of growth and development of Bhotia society, is calculated to provide a better insight into the dynamics of change in a tribal community and the various socio-cultural processes which help a community to adapt to such changes. Useful data have also been provided in numerous tables.

212   **Regional Fellowship Programme for National Personnel Responsible for Planning and Organizing Disability Prevention and Rehabilitation Services.**
Bangkok: ESCAP, 1987. 46p.

This seminar was held in Manila between 9 and 27 June 1986. The pamphlet provides information on subjects such as community participation in helping and caring for disabled people, and rehabilitation and training programmes for disabled people in Asia, particularly in Bhutan, China, Malaysia, the Philippines, Samoa and Thailand.

213   **The tribes and castes of Bengal; ethnographic glossary.**
Herbert Hope Risley.   Calcutta: Bengal Secretariat Press, 1892. 2 vols.

A detailed introduction to the tribes, castes and hill tribes is followed by a listing in dictionary form of the various groups of people forming the population of Bengal. The larger segments of the populace receive considerable attention. For example, there is an eight-page entry in Volume 2 under 'Lepcha', covering the origin of the people, physical type, structure of the tribe, marriage, inheritance, religion, food, dress, and occupation. The Lepchas are a Mongolian tribe who form a large part of the population of Sikkim, Darjeeling and Bhutan.

214 **Determinants of modernization and human response in the Eastern Himalayas.**
Harvir Sharma. In: *The Himalayas: profiles of modernisation and adaptation*, edited by S. K. Chaube. New Delhi: Sterling, 1985, p. 10-16.

This chapter covers the eastern part of Nepal, Sikkim and Bhutan. It contains a general introduction to the physical set-up of the area: the use of land, mountain and forests; the type of people inhabiting the area; the major religions (Buddhism and Hinduism); power projects included in Bhutan's Third Five-Year Plan (1971-76); transport facilities and development of roads; modernization in the field of science and technology; mineral resources and the extent of industrialization. The author concludes that: the level of industrialization in the area is fairly poor; modern transport routes are facilitating increased trade in goods; development and modernization efforts are concentrated only in the valleys which have electric power; and political decisions have not been taken to eradicate poverty from the areas which are rich in natural resources.

215 **The Bhutanese urban perspective.**
A. C. Sinha. In: *South Asian experience*, edited by R. C. Sharma. New Delhi: Criterion, 1988, p. 85-95.

The papers in this volume cover urban trends, problems, and the issues confronting the countries of Bangladesh, Bhutan, India, Nepal, Pakistan and Sri Lanka. The aim is to help to develop a proper understanding of the South Asian environment. This particular paper provides, firstly, a brief survey of the Bhutanese economy, the pattern of authority, and the social structure. Secondly, it reports on the geographical setting in which the major urban centres are located. Next, it analyses the nature and functions of the two sets of Bhutanese cities in the inner Himalayas and the foothills, and lastly, it examines the structure, organization and role of the cities in the Bhutanese national experience.

Politics and Government

216 Government and politics in South Asia.
    Craig Baxter, Yogendra K. Malik, Charles H. Kennedy, Robert C.
    Oberst.   Lahore, Pakistan: Vanguard, 1988. 415p.
On pages 363-7 the book contains background information on Bhutan, and provides
useful information on the ethnic composition of the population, on political
developments in the country from 1907 to 1971, and on its modernization programme.
It also includes Indo-Bhutan relations from 1947 to 1971, by which time Bhutan, with
Indian support, had become a member of the UNO and other international
organizations.

217 Bhutan.
    Gudrun Dalibor.   *Asia and Pacific Review* (1985), p. 105-6.
Dalibor provides information on the present conditions in Bhutan. The article covers:
Bhutan's efforts to assert its independence in its relations with other countries;
liberalization of the political and economic system of the country; a regular air service
between Calcutta and Paro; the economy of the country; foreign aid from both India
and the UN; shortage of trained and skilled manpower; signs of reduced dependence
on India; and the resumption of relations between Bhutan and China. This information
is followed by a very useful 'Business Guide' to Bhutan.

218 Diarchy in Bhutan: the Dharma Raja Deb Raja system.
    A. Deb.   *Bengal Past and Present*, vol. 91, no. 172 (July-Dec. 1972),
    p. 158-65.
Deb provides information on the system of government in Bhutan between 1772 and
1865, when two persons were jointly vested with supreme powers. At the head of the
Bhutan government there were nominally two supreme authorities: the Dharma Raja,
known as Shaptrung Renipoche, the spiritual head; and the Deb or Depa Raja, the
temporal ruler. The Dharma Raja is regarded as a very high incarnation of Buddha,
but sometimes owing to the failure to discover a reincarnation after the death of
Dharma Raja, Deb Raja held both offices. The office of Deb Raja was usually held for

Politics and Government

three years, having been elected by the council, consisting of Dharma Raja, Deb Raja and other subordinate officials. The author outlines the functions of each office and concludes that these two authorities usually fought with each other in order to increase their power.

219 **World encyclopedia of political systems.**
Edited by George E. Delury.   Harlow, England: Longman, 1983. 2 vols.

Volume 2 provides, on pages 1235-6, a brief political and general history of Bhutan, together with a short description of its population, its legal system, and the government efforts for economic, political and social development.

220 **Bhutan, kham and the upper Assam line.**
A. R. Field.   *Orbis*, vol. 3 (Summer 1959), p. 180-92.

Field explains the political situation of Bhutan, Nepal and Sikkim in 1950, and points out the strategic importance of Bhutan to India. He also explains briefly the Indian position over Chinese claims to large areas of Indian territory and to some parts of Bhutan, Sikkim and Nepal.

221 **The making of modern Tibet.**
A. Tom Grunfeld.   London: Zed Books, 1987. 277p. map. bibliog.

This book is a study of Tibetan refugees and China. It examines their conflicting claims in the light of archival material. Pages 186-7, 201-2 and 218-19 cover the history of Tibetan refugee settlement in Bhutan; the reasons behind the tension between the Government of Bhutan and the refugees; a plot to assassinate the heir of Bhutan and turn Bhutan into a military camp and a staging area for raids into neighbouring China; and American views on the problem. In all, it is a useful study on the refugee problem in Bhutan.

222 **Political problems of Bhutan.**
D. B. Gurung.   *United Asia*, vol. 12, no. 4 (1960), p. 368-9.

Gurung provides a brief survey of the political history of Bhutan from 1907 to 1960, and attacks the political system where the King has absolute powers and its people are deprived of all civil and political rights. He concludes that as long as the people are deprived of their rights, the political condition of the country will remain unstable and economic progress will remain at a standstill.

223 **Bhutan's strategic environment: changing perceptions.**
Manorma Kohli.   *India Quarterly*, vol. 42, no. 2 (1986), p. 142-53.

Kohli examines the geopolitical significance of Bhutan, from the 1960s to 1985, and its efforts to assert its independence from India and China. In 1971 Bhutan became a member of the United Nations, and subsequently became a member of the non-aligned movement. In the 1970s Bhutan sought to reduce its economic dependence on India by establishing new trading relations, including closer ties with China. Growing rapprochement between India and China since 1979 has allowed Bhutan to expand its economic and diplomatic relations beyond its two large neighbours without sacrificing its national security interests.

224 **Le Bhoutan ou un Royaume Bouddhiste dans l'Himalaya.** (Bhutan, or a Buddhist kingdom in the Himalayas.)
Alain Lamballe. *Afrique et l'Asie Modernes (France)*, vol. 3 (1979), p. 1-19.
This article provides information on Bhutan's slow progress towards modernization and its efforts to gain freedom from India's control in the 20th century.

225 **Recent trends in Bhutanese politics.**
R. C. Mishra. *South Asian Studies*, vol. 12, no. 1-2 (1977), p. 132-44.
Mishra examines the politics of Bhutan during the previous two decades, and in particular its relations with India and China, difficulties in handling a large population of Tibetan and Nepalese origin with limited economic resources, and the need for the modernization of agriculture and power sources.

226 **The government and politics of Tibet.**
Ram Rahul. New Delhi: Vikas, 1969. 160p.
This is the first detailed study – and probably the most thorough available source – on the subject of the government and politics of Tibet. Pages 102-5 cover Buddhism in Bhutan (1594-1651); the civil war which raged in Bhutan over the question of the Shabdrung Rimpoche (1728-30); Anglo-Bhutanese conflicts of 1838-39 and 1864-65; the institution of Shabdrung Rimpoche in Bhutan like that of the Dalai Lama in Tibet; and suzerainty of Tibet over Bhutan. The foreword of the book was written by the Dalai Lama on 27 June 1969.

227 **System of administration in the Himalaya.**
Ram Rahul. *Asian Survey*, vol. 9, no. 9 (Sept. 1969), p. 694-702.
This article examines briefly the nature of the frontier character of the Himalaya which has always conditioned the system of administration in Bhutan, Nepal and Sikkim. Rahul also discusses briefly the administrative reorganization of the North-East Frontier Agency, which includes Bhutan, Ladakh and other hill areas, as well as giving some information about the Indian Frontier Administrative Service.

228 **The buffer states of Sikkim and Bhutan.**
E. H. Rawlings. *Eastern World*, vol. 16, no. 11 (Nov. 1962), p. 12-13.
Rawlings provides a brief survey of the history, economic conditions, and economic development programmes initiated by the Indian Government in the state of Sikkim and Bhutan in 1962. The article concludes that there is an anti-Indian section within the Bhutanese ruling class which favours close contacts with China, and that they are prepared to accept aid from China, and would probably force the Bhutan Government to do so. Nevertheless, there is a strong Chinese influence in Bhutan, especially in cultural and religious spheres.

229 **The politics of Bhutan.**
Leo E. Rose. London: Cornell University Press, 1977. 237p. map. bibliog.
A useful contribution by a scholar from the University of California at Berkeley about the politics of a country which is not very well known to the outside world. The work is based on personal interviews with the Bhutanese people, and it includes the following

Politics and Government

chapters: Historical and social heritage; Foreign relations; Neutralizing the external environment; Politics and public policy; Constitutional system and national political institutions; Administration in Bhutan; The process of change. A glossary is included of useful terms used in the book.

230 **Bhutan: the dragon kingdom in crisis.**
Nari Rustomji. Delhi: Oxford University Press, 1978. 150p. map.

The author of the book was a close friend of the Royal family of Bhutan. He examines the evolution of the government from primitive, spiritual and temporal to the democratic formation of the Assembly. In 1953 Jigme Dorji, a progressive Prime Minister, established the first Tsongdu (Assembly) in the country. The Assembly consists both of elected representative and of nominees of the King and has complete freedom of discussion. The proceedings are conducted in Dzonghka (the official language of Bhutan which has close affinities with Tibetan). The book also examines the tension between the Royal family and the Prime Minister, the crisis created by the assassination of the Prime Minister on 5 April 1964, and the consequent proceedings of the trial for treason of Brigadier Namgyal (Chief of the Army Staff) who was an accomplice to the assassin, Mr Jambey, and three others.

231 **Visit to Bhutan by the Chairman of Palestine Liberation Organization.**
Kuensel, vol. 20, no. 17 (28 April 1985), p. 2-6.

The Chairman of the PLO, Yasser Arafat, visited Thimphu (Bhutan) on 21-22 April 1985. *Kuensel*'s special correspondent discusses the purpose of Arafat's visit, and mentions the formalities observed on his arrival and the places shown to him. It also gives a brief political biography of Arafat and his views on the Israel–Palestine conflict.

Legal Statutes

232 **Disciplinary code.**
  Drafted by Colonel S. S. Bedi, assisted by V. P. Singh, C. M. Pahuja, S. D. Sharma. Thimpu: Government of Bhutan, 1981. 124, 192, 60p.
An army act and the King's procedural regulations for the Royal Bhutanese army.

233 **Livestock Act.**
  Thimpu: Royal Government of Bhutan, 1980. 37p.
A draft livestock act and by-laws of the Kingdom of Bhutan, issued by the Ministry of Development, Animal Husbandry Department.

Foreign Relations

234 Prospects of Bangladesh-Bhutan relations.

Kamal Uddin Ahmed.   In: *Bangladesh – global politics*, edited by
S. R. Chakravarty, Virendra Narain.   New Delhi: South Asian
Publishers, 1988, p. 170-81.

The author, Professor of Politics at the University of Dhaka, examines the cordial
relationship between Bangladesh and Bhutan in the context of the South Asian
Association for Regional Cooperation (SAARC). The economic and political
relationship between the two countries is examined between 1974 and 1987, and their
agreement on trade is given in full.

235 Select documents on India's foreign policy and relations 1947-1972.

A. Appadorai.   Delhi: Oxford University Press, 1982. 2 vols.

The emphasis in this selection of documents is on India's foreign relations, as
distinguished from foreign policy. Whatever the policy may be, it is in the bilateral and
multilateral relations of countries that it is implemented, and the success of the policy
determined. Out of 316 documents, 238 relate to India's foreign relations, and 145 out
of the 238 bear on India's relations with her neighbours. India's foreign relations with
Bhutan are mentioned in volume 1 on pages 498-9, 547-8, 569-70, and 627-8.
Elsewhere in this volume Appadorai refers to Bhutan and highlights the views of the
Chinese Foreign Office.

236 Bhutan: a geopolitical survey.

Major R. Avtar.   In: *India's Northern security (including China, Nepal
and Bhutan),* edited by Gautam Sharma, K. S. Nagar.   New Delhi:
Reliance, 1986, p. 193-200.

The aim of this paper is to examine and assess the geopolitical situation of Bhutan and
its relations with India from the 18th century, when Bhutan was a theocracy, up to
1984. The themes in the article are: the historical background of Bhutan; relations
between Bhutan and India; and why Bhutan is breaking away from India.

237 India's economic and political relations with Bhutan.
Valentine J. Belfiglio. *Asian Survey*, vol. 12 (Aug. 1972), p. 676-85.
This article provides useful information about India's role in the economic and political development of Bhutan, and also explains the current situation on defence agreement and trade relations between these two countries.

238 The battle of NEFA: the undeclared war.
G. S. Bhargava. Bombay: Allied Publishers, 1964. 187p. map.
The author was a special correspondent for the *Hindustan Times* in 1960 and was posted at NEFA (North-East Frontier Agency of India). Bhargava provides an historical survey of the Indo-Chinese rivalry at NEFA. On pages 12, 13, 48-51 and 110-13 he discusses Chinese intentions with regard to Bhutan, the influx of Tibetan refugees into Bhutan, and the implications of the rivalry between India and China.

239 India and China.
Sudhakar Bhat. New Delhi: Popular Book Services, 1967. 260p. map.
This volume begins with the phase of friendship and the border problem between India and China. It describes the strategic importance of Tibet, Bhutan and Sikkim to both the countries, and the respect and importance, especially to India, of the McMahon Line which has been violated by the Chinese. This line is 830 miles long, extending westwards from the tri-junction of India, Burma and Tibet up to the north-eastern tip of Bhutan. The line was not drawn by McMahon (Sir Arthur Henry McMahon, political adviser to the Viceroy of India), but at the Simla conference which he convened. The long-existing boundary line along the highest watershed ridge was merely accepted and formalized. On pages 49-53 Bhat provides information on Bhutan-Indian roads, a treaty of their good relations, teaching of Hindi in Bhutanese schools, and the appointment of a Director-General of Development in Bhutan.

240 'Intrusions' into Bhutan – spotlight on China's tactics.
R. K. Chattarjee. *Tibetan Review*, vol. 14, no. 10 (Oct. 1979), p. 25-7.
Chattarjee emphasizes that the reported intrusion of the Chinese and Tibetan graziers into Bhutanese territory is in line with the Chinese style of raising border issues with neighbouring countries. During such incursions, the intruders usually have the support of the Chinese Frontier Guards. He also gives a history of Chinese violations of neighbouring territories. The Chinese claim that the allegations are not true and that the 'violations' may be attributed to the fact that Chinese surveyors are taking a look at the China-Bhutan boundary.

241 India-Bhutan relationship: some new trends.
T. K. Roy Choudhury. *World Today*, vol. 37, no. 12 (Dec. 1981), p. 476-81.
The author examines Indo-Bhutan relations from 1949 to 1980 together with the economic aid Bhutan has received from India towards its modernization. Roy Choudhury argues that, although Indian aid has been helpful to Bhutan, it has not made Bhutan strictly observe the Indo-Bhutan treaty of 1949. Although fully independent, Bhutan agreed in a treaty of 1949 to be guided by the Government of India in regard to its external affairs. Some new trends in Bhutan's perception of its existing ties with India are now manifest in various acts ranging from its behaviour at

the United Nations to demands for the revision of the treaty. For its part, the Indian Government has shown a generally relaxed attitude, at least in public, to Bhutan's bid for greater autonomy.

242 A brief study of the Bhutan-Tibet relations.
Srikant Dutt. *Tibetan Review*, vol. 13, no. 11 (Nov. 1978), p. 12-15.

This is an attempt to explain the history of the estranged relations between Bhutan and Tibet. These two countries have a long history of bilateral relations (political, economic and cultural), but their relations came to their lowest level when some Tibetan refugees in Bhutan were charged by the Royal Government with complicity in a plot against the present king. The author believes that in the aftermath of 1974 the Tibetan refugees were subjected to various forms of persecution, and in March 1977 the Indian Government intervened and the relations between the Bhutan Government and Tibetan refugees started to improve.

243 India and the Himalayan states.
Srikant Dutt. *Asian Affairs*, vol. 11, no. 1 (1980), p. 71-81.

The Himalayan states of Bhutan, Nepal, and Sikkim have been buffer states for India since the 18th century. Sikkim had long been treated as an Indian state, but on 14 April 1975 a referendum was held in Sikkim and the state became a part of India. In the 1950s Prime Minister Nehru's attitude toward these states was distinctly paternalistic. Since 1947 the Himalayan states have remained subservient to India, which has been unwilling to yield the 'inherited' colonial right to these lands.

244 Cooperation and conflict in South Asia.
Partha S. Ghosh. New Delhi: Manohar, 1989. 265p. bibliog.

Ghosh analyses the foreign relations of India with South Asian countries. Chapter five (p. 136-53) deals with India-Bhutan relations. It introduces the reader to the history and political system of Bhutan and the historical background of the Indo-Bhutanese relations. The treaty of 1949 between the two countries and their foreign relations from 1949 to 1987 are also analysed. The author concludes that Bhutan has neither so far posed any serious challenge to Indian foreign policy and strategic planning, nor has it put forward an earnest demand for the revision of the 1949 treaty, but the good relations between the countries cannot last long as a result of Chinese influence in the area.

245 The hills of India.
Henry Gibbs. London: Jarrolds, 1961. 254p.

This brief study about the hill countries – Afghanistan, West Pakistan, Kashmir, Nepal, Assam and India – discusses Bhutan and its foreign relations with India and China – on pages 184-90. It also provides a picture of the geopolitical area which may convey something of its atmosphere and the life of its people, and of its possible weaknesses.

246 **Prelude to India: a study of India's relations with Himalayan states.**
Narendra Goyal. New Delhi: Cambridge Book and Stationery Store, 1964. 179p.
There are ten chapters in this book which deals primarily with Indo-Nepal relations after 1947. They include some discussion of India's relations with China, Tibet, Sikkim and Bhutan.

247 **H. E. Mr. Rajiv Gandhi visits Bhutan.**
Kuensel (Special issue, Oct. 1985), p. 1-13.
The traditional bonds of friendship between Bhutan and India stem from the compulsions of geography and their shared heritage of ancient history and culture. In more recent times, the bonds have been based on the close personal friendship and mutual affection between Rajiv Gandhi and King Jigme Singye Wangchuck of Bhutan. This whole issue of *Kuensel* gives an account of Gandhi's goodwill visit to Bhutan from 25 September to 1 October 1985, and his various speeches in which he underlined that the Indian economic cooperation with Bhutan is based on the sharing of resources rather than aid or assistance. He also made clear the Indian Government's views that Bhutan should remain an independent country, choosing its own way of life and taking the path of progress according to its own will. About three pages of the issue are devoted to Mrs Gandhi's achievements as Prime Minister of India, and to the description of a ceremony in which Mrs Gandhi was posthumously given Bhutan's highest national award, the 'Druk Wangyal' as a token of great esteem and deep appreciation for her personal contribution to Indo-Bhutan friendship.

248 **India and the China crisis.**
Steven A. Hoffmann. Berkeley, California: University of California Press, 1990. 324p. bibliog.
This is a major contribution to the analysis of the continuing conflict between India and China. It also provides a valuable study of how states behave in a foreign policy crisis. Pages 66-7 offer a straightforward account of the foreign relations of India and China in relation to Bhutan. Hoffmann also provides the 1959 statements of PM Nehru and PM Chou En-lai on Bhutan's borders.

249 **Roads and rivals: the political uses of access in the borderlands of Asia.**
Mahnaz Z. Ispahani. Ithaca, New York; London: Cornell University Press, 1989. 286p. 12 maps. bibliog.
Ispahani examines the critical importance of routes to developing nation-states and offers an insight into the relationships between technology, evolution of political interests and national identity. On pages 178-81, he examines the strategic importance of Bhutan to India and the reasons behind the Indian Government's building of roads in Bhutan.

250 **China South Asian relations 1947-1980.**
Edited by R. K. Jain. New Delhi: Radiant, 1981. 2 vols.
This is a study of 973 documents, from 1947 to 1980, which deal with the political, economic and military facets of China's relations with South Asia. The documents, both in the original English and translated from Chinese into English, provide the full text of all important trade, economic and cultural agreements and joint communiqués. There are 20 pages on Bhutan on account of the important Tibet-Bhutan border. The

Foreign Relations

Chinese claim that India has no right to announce its protectorate over Bhutan, while the Indian Government disagrees that the frontier east of Bhutan as shown on the Chinese map is the traditional frontier.

251 Bhutan and Sikkim: Himalayan Shangri-La, now darkened by communist China's shadow, faces up to the 20th century.
Pradyumna P. Karan. *Canadian Geographical Journal,* vol. 65, no. 6 (Dec. 1962), p. 201-9.

Karan provides a short review of the political situation of Bhutan and Sikkim in the early 1960s and their relations with India, China and the rest of the world at that time. The article is well documented with photographs of people, market scenes, monasteries, and labourers working on the roads.

252 Geo-political structure of Bhutan.
Pradyumna P. Karan. *Indian Quarterly*, vol. 19, no. 3 (July-Sept. 1963), p. 203-13.

The kingdom of Bhutan, on the borders of India and China, has been a focus of great attention in view of the Sino-Indian border dispute. Bhutan abandoned its policy of isolation after the Chinese take-over of Tibet. Bhutan's policy of modernization, with the help of India, is discussed, together with physical and economic features of Bhutan. Karan also highlights the special relationship of India with Bhutan on the basis of mutual trust and friendship.

253 The security of Southern Asia.
D. E. Kennedy. London: Chatto & Windus for the Institute for Strategic Studies, 1965. 308p.

Pages 205-8 are about Bhutan and cover the period 1960-63. Kennedy analyses India-China rivalry on the Bhutan and Sikkim borders. India claims to have a special relationship with Bhutan, and it has claimed the right to include the northern borders of Bhutan and Sikkim in any Sino-Indian agreement. China refused to discuss with India the Tibetan borders of Bhutan and Sikkim, on the grounds that they were not a part of India. Mr Nehru declared that a Chinese entrance into Sikkim (a part of India) and Bhutan would be regarded by India as an act of aggression by the Chinese. The author believes that India would have a problem in defending Bhutan, once the Chinese had invaded it from Tibet, because of the difficult mountain and jungle terrain.

254 The China factor in Indo-Bhutanese relations.
Manorma Kohli. In: *Studies in India's foreign policy*, edited by Surendra Chopra. Amritsar, India: Guru Nanak Dev University, 1983, p. 160-70.

This article examines the history of relations between India-Bhutan and China. It describes how the present Indo-Bhutanese relations are governed by the treaty of 1949, and that this treaty was largely based on the treaty of 1910 signed between the British India Government and Bhutan. It is the strategic location of Bhutan which makes it obligatory for India to have friendly and intimate relations with that country. In 1959 China occupied Tibet, and Bhutan was looked upon as part of Tibet, a view by which the Bhutanese felt threatened. They therefore started leaning towards India for help and development. The good relations between Bhutan and Tibet from the seventh century onwards are also discussed.

255 **Chinese interest in Bhutan: evolution of the British Indian perspective.**
Manorma Kohli. *China Report*, vol. 19, no. 4 (1983), p. 37-45.
The author discusses Chinese attempts to extend their suzerainty to Bhutan and other Himalayan states, and the British Indian reaction to these initiatives. The Chinese had always assumed that control over these border areas was their legitimate heritage, but the British felt that Asian stability was best served if the Himalayas marked the southern boundary of Chinese influence. The British were able to take the steps necessary to realize their objectives by using Tibet as the keystone of their policies.

256 **Bhutan: thoughts of sovereignty.**
K. Krishna Moorthy. *Far Eastern Economic Review*, vol. 31 (16 Feb. 1961), p. 295-7.
The author examines the position of Bhutan as a buffer state and describes the importance of Bhutan in international relations. He also describes the efforts of Bhutan to be more independent from Indian government.

257 **Documents on Indian affairs 1960.**
Edited by Girja Kumar, V. K. Arora. London: Asia Publishing House, 1964. 636p.
This volume comprises select documents on India's internal and external affairs for the year 1960. On pages 335-8 it discusses whether Bhutan can defend its border against any external threat, and a proposal of a comprehensive defence treaty with India for stationing an Indian army contingent in Bhutan. Some extracts are reproduced from the text of a Press conference on 16 March 1960 of Druk Gyalpo and Prime Minister Jigme Dorji of Bhutan. On pages 501-4 there is the reproduction of a note sent to China by the Government of India on the Bhutan and Sikkim border dispute with China.

258 **India and Bhutan.**
Kapileshwar Labh. New Delhi: Sindu, 1974. 275p. bibliog.
This is a revised and enlarged version of the author's PhD thesis at the Indian School of International Studies, now a part of the Jawaharlal Nehru University. The author claims that it is the first comprehensive study of Indo-Bhutanese relations in modern times. The author tries to show that Indian relations with Bhutan were at first based on the commercial interests of the British East India Company, and the issue of Bhutanese incursions into the Indian territories, and it was only later that Chinese foreign policy towards Tibet and India influenced India policy towards Bhutan. The work includes Indo-Bhutan relations after 1947, and an account of Bhutan as an independent country from 1947 to 1972.

259 **The international status of Bhutan before 1947.**
Kapileshwar Labh. *International Studies*, vol. 13, no. 1 (1974), p. 75-93.
Labh outlines the history of Bhutan's foreign relations with India, China, and British colonialism, 1890-1911. The article includes the Indo-Bhutanese treaty of 1910.

Foreign Relations

260 **The McMahon Line: a study in the relations between India, China and Tibet, 1904-1914.**
Alastair Lamb.   London: Routledge & Kegan Paul; Toronto: University of Toronto Press, 1966. 2 vols. 656p.

A very useful reference work which covers all aspects of foreign relations between India, China, Tibet and Bhutan. From 1907 onwards Mr Chang Yin-tang of China began to show a close interest in Bhutanese affairs and the British Indian Government became increasingly alarmed about Chinese plans to grab Tibet, Bhutan and Nepal. They opposed China's attempts to grab Tibet and Bhutan – Nepal could defend itself at that time. Consideration is also given to the diplomatic and military devices used in the past to establish spheres of influence in Bhutan which had been a continual threat to the peace of the northern frontier of India. Lamb also discusses all the British missions to Bhutan and examines the Anglo-Bhutanese treaties of 1865 and 1910. There are several pages on Bhutan, but the important material is on pages 158-68, 265-8, 278-82 and 292-5. The McMahon Line is the Indo-Chinese border-line, drawn in 1914 at a British-Tibetan-Chinese conference and named after a British administrator. Communist China, which has absorbed Tibet, repudiated the McMahon Line as delimiting her border with India. India insists that it is a legitimate and legal border-line.

261 **Tibet, China and India 1914-1950: a history of Imperial diplomacy.**
Alastair Lamb.   Hertingfordbury, England: Roxford Books, 1989. 594p. bibliog.

Lamb offers an extremely useful account of Imperial diplomacy and the foreign relations of Tibet-China-India between 1914 and 1950. The book is a good introduction to the Indo-Bhutanese-Chinese boundary issue and the border questions – the McMahon Line and the Assam Himalayas, 1914-36, and North-East Frontier Agency, 1936-45. These are mainly discussed on pages 401-523.

262 **Bhutan and Sikkim: two buffer states.**
Werner Levi.   *World Today*, vol. 15, no. 12 (Dec. 1959), p. 492-500.

Levi describes Bhutan and Sikkim as objects of continuous rivalry between India and China. The role of Bhutan and Sikkim as buffer states has become more significant after the Chinese takeover of Tibet. The author discusses whether the takeover of Tibet by China has enhanced the sense of insecurity in both Bhutan and Sikkim and so has led them to depend heavily on India for their security.

263 **The defence and foreign policies of India.**
V. Longer.   London: Oriental University Press, 1988. 357p. bibliog.

This is a comparative study of the defence and foreign policies of post-independence India with special reference to Pakistan and China. The effect on India of the flow of American arms to Pakistan, the nuclear programme of Pakistan, and US-China and China-Pakistan military cooperation are all discussed. Pages 88-91, 276-8, 288-9 and 307-8 covers the excellent foreign relations between India and Bhutan, and how Bhutan solved its Tibet border problem with China. The conflict between the Bhutanese and their Nepalese inhabitants is also discussed. The author was a former adviser in the Indian Government.

264 **Sikkim and Bhutan: an historical conspectus.**
P. L. Mehra. *Journal of Indian History*, vol. 46, part 1-3 (April 1968), p. 89-124.

The relationship that exists between India and the Himalayan states of Sikkim and Bhutan has evolved over the years into something quite distinct and, in a manner of speaking, quite unique. At the time when the article was published Sikkim was a protectorate of India, but on 14 April 1975 a referendum was held in Sikkim and the people of the state overwhelmingly voted for a fully fledged statehood within India. The Constitution of India was amended to accommodate Sikkim as a state within the Union of India. Although Bhutan is a fully independent state, by a treaty of 1949, it agreed to be guided by the Government of India in regard to its external relations. In the 1960s the threat which Bhutan and Sikkim faced from China brought them closer to India. The article spells out the nature of the threat and views it against a brief historical background, but the author does not offer answers to the problem.

265 **Dhaka summit and SAARC: a broad overview.**
Pramod Kumar Mishar. Calcutta: Bagchi, 1986. 70p.

The author, Director of the Netaji Institute for Asian Studies, examines the prospects of the South Asian Association for Regional Cooperation (SAARC) in the light of India and Pakistan's misunderstanding and mistrust of each other. SAARC came into existence on 8 December 1985 when its charter was signed by Bangladesh, Bhutan, India, the Maldives, Nepal, Pakistan and Sri Lanka. The author assesses the failures and achievements of SAARC countries from 1981 to 1986.

266 **Bhutan-China relations.**
R. C. Misra. *China Report*, vol. 17, no. 2 (1980), p. 43-50.

Misra provides a review of China's past and present relations with Bhutan. This covers British policy towards Bhutan, Chinese reasons for seeking influence over that nation, British efforts to keep the Chinese at bay, Bhutanese hostility towards China, and the treaty of 1910, which limited Bhutan's autonomy. Following World War II, Bhutan endeavoured to maintain strong relations with Great Britain, especially after the Chinese revolution. The fall of Tibet has shown Chinese intentions, and caused a Western response which has emphasized the strategic importance of Bhutan.

267 **Bhutan steps out.**
S. D. Muni. *World Today*, vol. 40, no. 12 (Dec. 1984), p. 514-20.

The author, an Associate Professor at the Jawaharlal Nehru University, India, assesses and analyses the development of foreign relations between Bhutan and its neighbouring countries, including India, Nepal, Bangladesh and China. The major part of the article deals with: the Chinese threat to Bhutan and its insistence in dealing with Bhutan directly on border issues; why India has always refused to let China talk to Bhutan directly on Bhutan-China border issues; why Bhutan is slipping away from the influence of India and its objectives in talking directly to China on the boundary issues; the background of some of the internal problems of Bhutan which are caused by Nepali people, estimated to represent about 30 to 52 per cent of Bhutan's total population; and why Bhutan is now aiming for greater independence from India.

Foreign Relations

268 **India's foreign policy: selected speeches, September 1946-April 1961.**
Jawaharlal Nehru. New Delhi: Government of India, Publication
Division, 1961. 612p.

The material in this collection has been selected from the official record of the Prime
Minister's speeches and statements, both in India and abroad. The majority of the
speeches and addresses were delivered extempore. Pages 338-40 and 355-6 include a
statement in the Lok Sabha (Lower House of the Parliament) on 28 August 1959 on
Bhutanese defence, its political relations with both India and China, and the Indo-
Bhutanese boundary.

269 **Trans-Himalayan confrontation.**
Norman D. Palmer. *Orbis*, vol. 6, no. 4 (1963), p. 513-27.

This study covers the period from 1950 to 1962. A general background to the Indo-
Chinese confrontation in the Himalayan region is followed by an analysis of India and
China's foreign policy towards the region. In the Sino-Indian treaty regarding Tibet –
April 1954 – China endorsed the famous 'Panchsheel' (Five Principles of Peaceful
Coexistence) introduced by India. On 20 October 1962, when China launched a major
offensive against India in the North-East Frontier Agency (NEFA), India could not
understand the reasons of such an attack. The author believes that the answer was in a
Chinese map showing the stages of the expansion of the Chinese empire during the
Tang dynasty (618-907 AD). China laid claim to all of the Himalayan regions, including
the territory in dispute with India, as well as Nepal, Bhutan and some parts of northern
India south of the Himalayas. Chinese control over these regions was never more than
a shadowy one, but the fact that they were once regarded as part of the Chinese
empire has never been forgotten by the Chinese. The author concludes that this new
crisis may be disastrous for India's future, but on the other hand, it may bring out the
best in Indian character and traditions, and the Indian nation may emerge from the test
with greater unity and vigour.

270 **China, Nepaul, Bhutan, and Sikkim: their mutual relations as set forth
in Chinese official documents.**
E. H. Parker. *Journal of the Manchester Oriental Society*, vol. 1
(1911), p. 129-52.

This article explores relations with China from the earliest times through to the
nineteenth century, but with special emphasis on the eighteenth century. Footnote
citations are incomplete, with the title often being the only information given.

271 **Premier Chou's press conference in New Delhi.**
Peking Review, vol. 3, no. 18 (3 May 1971), p. 20-3.

This is a report by a Chinese journalist about the foreign relations between China and
India. In the report, Premier Chou En-lai said that China had no boundary dispute
with Sikkim and Bhutan, or between China and Bhutan, and that China and Sikkim do
not form a Sino-Indian border. He also pointed out that China respected India's good
relations with Bhutan and Sikkim and was concerned about their welfare.

272 **Bhutan's external relations with India.**

T. T. Poulouse. *International and Comparative Law Quarterly* (London), vol. 20, pt. 2 (April 1971), p. 195-212.

This learned article discusses: the British India background; independent India's Himalayan policy; the 1949 Indo-Bhutan treaty; Chinese territorial claims on Bhutan's territory; and Bhutan's efforts to function as sovereign state in international relations, even though India is responsible for Bhutan's foreign affairs. The author advocates that India should sponsor Bhutan's name for United Nations membership.

273 **The Himalaya as a frontier.**

Ram Rahul. New Delhi: Vikas, 1978. 154p.

The author claims that this book is the first of its kind to deal with the frontier countries of Bhutan, the Tibet region of China, and the Sikkim region of India and Nepal. He analyses the relations that Tibet, Sikkim, Nepal and Bhutan have maintained between themselves and also their relations with India and China. The work focuses on the role of the Bon, Buddhist and Hindu religions in the history and politics of these countries. Bon was the religion of Tibet before the advent of Buddhism there. The book concludes with certain observations on the trends now discernible in the situation in the Himalaya. Pages 75-95 are relevant to Bhutan.

274 **The Himalaya borderland.**

Ram Rahul. Delhi: Vikas, 1970. 157p. bibliog.

This survey is intended for the general reader. It studies the southern half of the Himalayan borderland – Bhutan, Sikkim, Nepal, Uttarkhand (India), Lahul and Spiti (India) and Ladakh. On Bhutan it provides information on the life of its people; agriculture and climatic conditions; a brief history from the earliest times to 1964; monarchy and administration; and development efforts. The relevant pages are 10-12, 53-66, 111-13 and 123-7.

275 **The Himalayan frontier policy of India – a historical perspective.**

Rama T. S. Rao. *Indian Yearbook of International Affairs*, vol. 15-16 (1970), p. 558-67.

This is a critical study of India's post-independence border policy, a policy which departed from the flexible and pragmatic approach of the British Indian Government. Because of the Sino-Soviet border, the Chinese threat to Indian border security has been reduced, but China's relationship with Pakistan and its claim to the territories of Bhutan and Nepal could pose a military threat to India in the long run.

276 **Indo-Bhutanese relations.**

Laxman Singh Rathore. *Afro-Asian and World Affairs*, vol. 2 (1965), p. 360-8.

The whole of Bhutan presents a succession of lofty and rugged mountains running generally from north to south and separated by deep valleys. Its area is 18,000 square miles and the population in 1965 was about 300,000. Bhutanese people are Tibetan in stock, culture and outlook. The author provides a brief history of Bhutan and examines the Indo-Bhutanese relations from 1949 to 1965. Some information is also provided on Bhutan's boundary question with China, the Tibetan revolt against Chinese, and the assassination of the Prime Minister of Bhutan in 1964.

Foreign Relations

277 **Bhutan's external relations.**
Leo E. Rose. *Pacific Affairs*, vol. 47, no. 2 (Summer 1974), p. 192-208.

The author is a leading scholar on the Himalayan region, and in this article he describes the friendly relations between India and Bhutan, reviews Chinese border policy, and stresses the importance of Bhutan's emergence from isolation and alignment with India. Some information is also provided on the internal and external politics of Bhutan in the 1960s, and its admission to the United Nations in 1971 with the help of India. An attempt has also been made to study the foreign policies of China and Bhutan in establishing good relations between these two countries.

278 **The Himalayan border states: buffers in transition (Nepal, Sikkim and Bhutan).**
Leo E. Rose. *Asian Survey*, vol. 3, no. 2 (Feb. 1963), p. 116-21.

This is a succinct and penetrating analysis of domestic politics in Nepal, Sikkim and Bhutan and their foreign relations with India and China between 1960 and 1962. Some discussion as to how the Himalayan states of Nepal, Sikkim and Bhutan were surviving as autonomous political entities in spite of persistent attack from domestic critics is followed by an examination of the role of the Bhutanese State Congress, the only political party which represents the Nepali minority in Bhutan, a minority which was estimated to be about 25 per cent of Bhutan's population in 1962. The author also provides information on the Chinese invasion of India in October 1962 which brought virtually all internal politics in the border states to a halt. The article is somewhat dated, but perhaps a comparable situation still exists.

279 **Sino-Indian rivalry and the Himalayan border states.**
Leo E. Rose. *Orbis*, vol. 5, no. 2 (Summer 1961), p. 198-215.

Rose examines Sino-Indian rivalry in the Himalayan area (Nepal, Bhutan and Sikkim) from 1949 to 1961. He thinks that it is the most significant development in modern Asian international relations, and describes the international status of these states, and discusses their friendship treaties with India and China. He argues that the states had their treaty relations with India, but the treaty relations between the Ch'ing dynasty in China and the Gorkha dynasty in Nepal grew out of a power struggle between these two governments over Tibet during the last two decades of the eighteenth century. The author claims that there are no records of direct Chinese treaty relations with either Sikkim or Bhutan. Chinese assertions of past authority over these two states are based on supposed inheritance of rather vaguely defined Tibetan 'suzerain' rights. The author concludes that the motivations behind China's nefarious campaign to expand its influence across the great Himalayan barrier is still a subject for conjecture. The success of Chinese influence will depend upon the degree to which political leaders in the border states base their own policies on a correct appraisal of China's motivations and intentions.

280 **Bhutan: India's new partner in the third world.**
Seymour Scheinberg. *Journal of Indian History* (Golden Jubilee volume 1973), p. 761-74.

Scheinberg traces the cultural and political history of Bhutan from the 9th to the 20th century. Bhutan's relations with Tibet go back to the 9th century when missionaries spread Mahayana Buddhism in Tibet and Bhutan. Even though Bhutan sent an annual gift mission to Lhasa as a demonstration of respect from 1730 to 1950, Tibet never ruled Bhutan. British interest in Bhutan began in 1772. A second Bhutan War in 1864-65 brought significant British gains in access to the mountain kingdom, with guarantees of free trade and British arbitration on all border disputes. The Chinese and Tibetans in the second half of the 19th century attempted to oust British dominance in Bhutan but were unsuccessful. Control of Bhutan's foreign relations passed from England to India in 1947. Since the Chinese advance into Tibet in the 1950s Bhutan has become even more closely allied with India.

281 **Tibet disappears: a documentary history of Tibet's international status – the great rebellion and its aftermath.**
Compiled and edited by Chanakya Sen.   London: Asia Publishing House, 1960. 474p.

This volume offers a documentary account of the disappearing Tibet as told in treaties, discussions, resolutions, and statements by prominent men and organizations in India, China and at the United Nations. Page 51 gives the text of the treaty signed between Great Britain and Bhutan on 8 January 1910. Pages 388-93 include press reports of Chinese propaganda that Sikkim and Bhutan were part of the Chinese territory in the past, and were bound to return to the Chinese motherland within the next few years. Also included is the Chinese reply to India's protest and the discussion about it in the Indian Parliament.

282 **Area handbook for India.**
Rinn-Sup Shinn, John B. Folan, Marilyn G. Hopkins, Newton B. Parker, Robert L. Younglof.   Washington, DC: US Government Printing Office, 1970. 791p. bibliog.

The present volume is a revision of the *US Army Handbook for India*, prepared in 1963. On pages 402-3 it gives a brief history of the foreign relations of Bhutan and points out that Bhutan has long been a source of dispute between India and Communist China, but especially since the China pictorial map of July 1958 showed parts of Bhutan as belonging to China. There are also further analyses of the Chinese views about the border dispute.

283 **Jambudwipa: a blueprint for a South Asian community.**
V. Siddharthacharry.   London: Sangam, 1987. 461p.

On pages 231-4 and 246-9, the author deals with the plural society and ethnic divisions of Bhutan. Its relations with Tibet continued until it was invaded by the Chinese, but since the Tibetan royal families and Dalai Lama settled in India, the Bhutanese ruling dynasty are turning to India instead of Tibet as in the past. The short-term development of Bhutan by India and the good relations between the two countries are discussed, together with a comparison of monarchy in Nepal and Bhutan.

284 **Sikkim and Bhutan.**
Current Notes on International Affairs, vol. 33, no. 12 (Dec. 1962), p. 5-13.

The article, which comes from the Australian Department of External Affairs, emphasizes the strategic importance of Bhutan and Sikkim and presents the historical highlights and current position of Bhutan and Sikkim's economy, foreign relations and political structure.

Foreign Relations

285 Was the Simla convention not signed?
Nirmal C. Sinha. *Bulletin of Tibetology*, vol. 3, no. 1 (Feb. 1966), p. 33-8.

A. Henry McMahon, British government administrator, participated in the Simla Convention held in India in 1914, and a border-line called the McMahon Line was drawn and signed by the British, Tibetan and Chinese representatives. Communist China, which has absorbed Tibet, repudiated the McMahon Line as delimiting her border with India, while India insists that it is a legitimate and legal border-line. The McMahon Line is very important as it gives some protection to Bhutan from Chinese incursion into their territory. This article analyses and discusses the conference, provides different views on the subject, and leaves the reader to decide whether China is right in not agreeing to the boundary line.

286 India's northern security and Himalayan states.
Chitra Tiwari. *Asian Profile*, vol. 14, no. 5 (1986), p. 437-49.

After 1947, India tried to treat Bhutan, Sikkim and Nepal as semi-autonomous states, claiming that this was necessary for both their and India's security. In 1974, Sikkim became a part of India, and India made it clear that it would not allow intervention in the Himalayan states by other countries, a primacy which it continues to assert. The author also discusses India's intentions to see that these two states remain independent.

287 Treaty between India and Bhutan signed at Darjeeling, August 8, 1949.
Indian Year Book of International Affairs, 1953, p. 295-8.

Part III of this volume also contains the text of treaties concluded between India and other countries in the period between 1947 and 1952. The text of the treaty between the Government of India on one hand and His Highness the Druk Gyalpo's Government of Bhutan on the other is mentioned here. This yearbook is an annual publication of the University of Madras, India.

288 India's aid diplomacy in the Third World.
Dewan C. Vohra. Delhi: Vikas, 1980. 331p. bibliog.

This is an attempt to study India's massive aid programme to over a hundred countries of the southern hemisphere. One of the beneficiaries of India's aid programme amongst the Himalayan kingdoms is Bhutan. Indian aid to Bhutan was available from 1947 onwards – under the treaty of 1947 between these two countries – but it availed nothing until the Indian Prime Minister, Jawaharlal Nehru, visited the country in 1958. On pages 87-95, Vohra highlights the aid programme to Bhutan which includes construction of roads; deputations of experts; provision of training places for Bhutanese people; granting of scholarships to Bhutanese students to study in India; and the provision of equipment for projects undertaken in Bhutan.

Economy

289 **Basic documents of South Asian Regional Cooperation.**
New Delhi: Indian Ministry of External Affairs, Conference Cell, 1981.
89p.
Prepared for the SAARC, these documents – for the first South Asian Regional
Cooperation Meeting of Foreign Secretaries (21-23 April 1981 in Colombo) – provide a
clear and interesting picture of the intentions and role of SAARC in the economic
development of Bangladesh, Bhutan, India, the Maldives, Nepal, Pakistan and Sri
Lanka. The subjects covered in this document are: regional cooperation, economic
cooperation, social welfare of the SAARC countries, and how they can implement
these to their maximum benefit.

290 **Indian economic aid to Bhutan and Sikkim.**
Valentine J. Belfiglio. *International Studies*, vol. 13, no. 1 (1974),
p. 94-104.
Belfiglio offers an analysis of India's foreign aid to Bhutan and Sikkim for their
industrial, agricultural and economic development from 1954 to 1971.

291 **Planning strategy in Bhutan.**
S. S. Bhattacharya. In: *The Himalayas: profiles of modernisation and
adaptation*, edited by S. K. Chaube. New Delhi: Sterling, 1985.
p. 210-28.
This eighteenth chapter of the volume surveys India's active collaboration in the
economic and technical aid for accelerating the process of modernization of Bhutan's
roads, agriculture, industries, power (for the development of industry), and education.
Indian help in the development of Bhutan started in 1955, as a result of the Chinese
occupation of Tibet in 1950, and their claim, in 1954, of some 300 square miles of
Bhutanese territory. The impact of Indian aid to Bhutan is very encouraging and it will
help Bhutan in its progress towards all-round development.

Economy

292 **Bhutan abustle.**
Far Eastern Economic Review, vol. 42 (17 Oct. 1963), p. 144-6.

India was the chief architect and financier of the First Five-Year Development Plan of Bhutan (1961-66). With the help of India, Bhutan became a member of the Colombo Plan in 1962. This article, from a special correspondent, assesses the economic development of Bhutan between 1961 and 1963, and concludes that Bhutan should make more progress, as her leadership and people are energetic, and look forward to a better future.

293 **Bhutan: development in a Himalayan kingdom.**
Washington DC: World Bank, 1984. 177p. map. (World Bank Country Study).

Development efforts in Bhutan began in 1960, and since then the country has made much progress towards establishing a basic economic and social infrastructure, despite difficult physical conditions and a shortage of trained manpower. Bhutan joined the World Bank in 1981 and this is the first report by that institution on Bhutan. The report provides an overview of the economy and its current stage of development; the development strategy; the role of the country's economic institutions; government programmes to improve education and health standards; and the role of external assistance in development programmes in Bhutan.

294 **Bhutan: development planning in a unique environment.**
Washington, DC: World Bank, 1989. 109p.

This report is prepared by a team of World Bank economists who visited Bhutan in October and November of 1987. The report was revised in May 1988, following discussions with the Government of Bhutan in April 1988. The purpose of the report is to provide an understanding of the development potential and the development problems of Bhutan as it starts the implementation of its Sixth Five-Year Plan (1987/88–1991/92). It provides background information on the country's economy, agriculture, forestry, manufacturing and mining, power, roads and water supply, communications and tourism, education and health. It also highlights the economic development, together with a description of current conditions and policies, and forecasts of future trends. The long-term issues of development in Bhutan with regard to its scarce land resources, together with the need for foreign aid and for improved foreign aid coordination, are also discussed. As a result of its independent policy, development in Bhutan has been remarkably free from serious economic, social and cultural disruption.

295 **Bhutan feels its way.**
Eastern Economist, vol. 73, no. 26 (28 Dec. 1979), p. 1268–9.

The general correspondent of the journal provides information on the economic development programmes in Bhutan and its foreign relations with India in the year 1979. The report records the Tibetan refugee problem in Bhutan, as well as its efforts towards agricultural development and towards the improvement of both the quality and the number of sheep and yak herds.

296 **Bhutan – outline of the 6th Five Year Plan objectives (1987–1991/92).**
Thimpu: Bhutan Planning Commission, 1988. 21p.
This is a straightforward account of the Five-Year Plan, including discussions on the development of the planning institutions, changes in philosophy and methods, and the effects of cultural and attitudinal factors. This pamphlet is generally optimistic about the outlook for the economic development of the country, although it does reveal some obstacles to development.

297 **Bhutan. United Nations Development Programme (UNDP): a profile of technical co-operation.**
Thimphu: Department of Information and Broadcasting, 1985. 50p.
Bhutan has asserted itself as a fully sovereign, independent state, becoming a member of the United Nations in 1971. This booklet outlines the technical cooperation ь.vcn to Bhutan in order to develop its economy. Efforts to develop a modern economy in Bhutan date from the early 1960s. While strongly dependent on foreign aid, it was determined to follow its own set of priorities, keep public finance on an even keel, build up a well-trained but lean bureaucracy, and prevent environmental damage from over-exploitation of the forests or uncontrolled growth of tourism.

298 **Growing co-operation with Bhutan.**
S. Kumar Dev. *Commerce*, vol. 136, no. 3487 (8 April 1978), p. 547-8.
In keeping with its policy of being helpful to its neighbours, India agreed in 1978 that Bhutan could sell its products to Third World countries directly, instead of through India. The author believes that this is a great departure from established arrangements and practices, and it will facilitate Bhutan's international trade, something which will, in its turn, help meet the country's development needs and promote its economic growth. The author also provides information on India's contribution, from 1953 onwards, to the social and economic development programmes in Bhutan.

299 **Twenty five years of development in Bhutan.**
D. N. S. Dhakal. *Mountain Research and Development*, vol. 7, no. 3 (1987), p. 219-21.
This article covers modernization and planning in Bhutan from 1961 to 1986, with the help of India and other friendly countries, such as Australia, Japan and Switzerland. The current economic conditions and development strategies are also analysed.

300 **Energy for mountain districts.**
Kathmandu: International Centre for Integrated Mountain Development, 1986. 40p.
Energy is an essential input to all productive economic activity and the process of economic development inevitably demands increasingly higher levels of energy consumption. Topics covered in this pamphlet, based on the International workshop on district energy planning and management for integrated mountain development (held 3-5 May 1986 in Kathmandu), include energy policy and planning; demand for fuelwood; and regional cooperation for the development of rural and mountain areas of Bangladesh, Bhutan, China, India, Nepal, Pakistan and Tibet.

Economy

301 **Fifth Plan discussions between the Royal Government of Bhutan and Government of India.**

Kuensel, vol. 20, no. 14 (7 April 1985), p. 5-6.

India was the sole financier and architect of the First Five-Year Development Plan of Bhutan started in 1961. Since then, the Plans have continued for the economic development and modernization of the country. This article discusses the friendship between the two countries, financial help from India to Bhutan, and the economic progress due to planning. The article also includes some discussions on projects outside the Plan subsidy: river training to be established at Phuntsholing and Gaylegphug, and the community and sports stadium to be completed before the SAARC games in 1987. At the end it gives the names of the delegates of Bhutan and India who participated in the discussions.

302 **Final documents of the Second Meeting of Heads of State of SAARC.**

Bangalore, India: South Asian Association for Regional Cooperation, 1986. 44p.

This contains the text of the final documents of the second meeting of SAARC countries – South Asian Association for Regional Cooperation Meeting of Heads of State or Government (held on 16-17 November 1986 in Bangalore, India). The SAARC countries comprise Bhutan, Bangladesh, India, the Maldives, Nepal, Pakistan and Sri Lanka, and the documents are concerned with mutual help, development and economic cooperation.

303 **The Himalayan dilemma: reconciling development and conservation.**

Jack D. Ives, Bruno Messerli. London; New York: Routledge, 1989. 295p. bibliog.

The authors are leading experts on mountain environment and have an intimate knowledge of the Himalayan region. They have analysed the problems of the Himalayan region and demonstrated that their roots are basically socio-economic and political rather than environmental. On Bhutan (pages 52-3, 229-32, 248-53) they have explained that the First Plan (1961-66) concentrated on the development of government departments and the construction of roads. The Second, Third and Fourth Plans were on the development of education, agriculture, electricity, various industries and major irrigation works. The government of Bhutan established a number of primary and secondary schools and also provided a number of scholarships for brighter students to study abroad. The Fifth Plan (1981-86) has brought some structural changes in bureaucracy by decentralizing the development administration into district commissioners who will decide, with the help of local people, upon the nature and quantity of aid required by the people in each district. The authors have also made some suggestions for overcoming problems.

304 **Bhutan: development amid environmental and cultural preservation.**

Pradyumna P. Karan with the collaboration of Shigeru Iijima, and cartography by Gyula Pauer. Tokyo: Institute for the Study of Languages and Cultures of Asia and Africa, 1987. 155p. maps. (Monumenta Serindica, no. 17).

The development programme in Bhutan which started in 1960 has greatly improved the country. In 1960, the journey from the Indian border to the capital of Bhutan (Thimphu) took six days by mule, while at present the trip by car can be made in about five hours, and, since 1983, a regular air service between Calcutta and Paro takes only one and a half hours. From 1961 to 1962 Bhutan started modernization with a series of five-year development plans. This book is a study of patterns of development; land use and agriculture; forest use and management; energy, mining and manufacturing; and transport, trade and tourism. It is also an introduction to the environment, culture and development of Bhutan, and reveals how the King of Bhutan is trying not to lose the nation's culture and traditions in the wake of modern developments.

305 **Bhutan: problems and policies.**

H. N. Misra. New Delhi: Heritage, 1988. 153p. bibliog.

This national assessment report on Bhutan is the outcome of the project sponsored by the International Institute for Environment and Development in London. Dr Misra not only assesses the housing conditions, land and settlement policies in Bhutan, but also gives a clear understanding of the socio-economic background of the people, national settlement policies, land management policies, shelter, infrastructure and services, and foreign assistance for the development of the country. The author also assesses the achievements of the government in terms of road-building, communication, transport, health, education and agriculture, achievements which were complemented by progress in the productive sectors. Accordingly, in the Fourth Five-Year Plan the development of cash crops and resource-based industries was encouraged and these have yielded quite good results.

306 **Regional co-operation in South Asia.**

S. D. Muni. New Delhi: National Publishing House, 1984. 212p.

This study covers the economic cooperation between Bangladesh, Bhutan, India, the Maldives, Nepal, Pakistan and Sri Lanka.

307 **Crisis, pseudocrisis or supercrisis: poverty, women and young people in the Himalaya. A survey of recent developments.**

David C. Pitt. *Mountain Research and Development*, vol. 6, no. 2 (May 1986), p. 119-31.

This is a useful survey of women and young people in the Himalayas. The author argues that in Bhutan and Nepal the major cause of poverty, deforestation and environmental degradation may be market factors rather than population pressure. The author concludes that young people cannot play their proper role in society and the economy on account of poverty.

308 **The development program in the Himalaya.**

Ram Rahul. *Asian Survey*, vol. 8, no. 8 (Aug. 1968), p. 666-77.

The Himalayan borderland, including Bhutan, Sikkim and Nepal, is one of the most underdeveloped parts of the world. The article provides an agreeable mixture of information about the British attitude towards the development of Bhutan, and the special efforts of the Indian Government towards its development between 1950 and 1967. A brief account of the progress of roads, transport, communication, agriculture, education and health is followed by a survey of the natural resources of Bhutan. A succinct and penetrating analysis of the economic progress in Nepal and Sikkim is also provided.

Economy

309 **Royal Government of Bhutan – Fifth Plan, 1981-1987: main document.**
Thimpu: Royal Government of Bhutan, Planning Commission, 1982.
134p.

The Fifth Plan represents a conscious, internally consistent and carefully thought-out programme for the most efficient exploitation of the country's resources. The basic aim of the Plan was to raise the standard of living of the people. For the people of Bhutan, planning is a charter of orderly progress. With its implementation, Bhutan has advanced yet another stage towards its goal of prosperity.

310 **Strategic developments in Bhutan.**
Seymour Scheinberg. *Military Review*, vol. 58, no. 1 (1978), p. 47-55.

Scheinberg outlines and discusses Bhutan's economic development since the 1950s and its effects on the country's military and political role in South Asia.

311 **SAARC from Dhaka to Kathmandu.**
Shankar Man Singh.   Kathmandu: Ratna Pustak Bhandar, 1987. 79p.

This booklet discusses and evaluates the regional economic cooperation between the SAARC countries – India, Bhutan, the Maldives, Nepal, Pakistan and Sri Lanka.

312 **Social and economic impact of tourism development on developing countries of the ESCAP region: report of seminar.**
Bangkok: Economic and Social Commission for Asia and the Pacific, 1985. 40p.

Financial assistance for this seminar – Seminar on Social and Economic Impact of Tourism Development on Developing Countries of the ESCAP Region (held 5-11 February 1985 in Singapore) – came from the Government of Japan. The seminar covers such topics as tourism, manpower needs, economic aspects, social aspects, economic development of developing countries (Bhutan, Burma, Fiji, India, Indonesia, Malaysia, the Maldives, Nepal, Pakistan, the Philippines, the Republic of Korea, and Samoa).

313 **South Asian Regional Cooperation Meeting of Foreign Ministers, Malé, 10-11 July 1984.**
Malé, Maldives: Ministry of Foreign Affairs, 1984. 57p.

The first meeting of SAARC Foreign Ministers was held in Colombo in 1981. This was only the second such meeting despite the fact that they had hoped to meet frequently to discuss their mutual problems and plan their strategy for economic development. The Ministers argued that the SAARC countries (Bangladesh, Bhutan, India, the Maldives, Pakistan, Nepal and Sri Lanka) would not solve their problems unless the meetings become a genuine part of a development programme. The main aim of SAARC is to help each other to develop economically.

314 **Statistical handbook of Bhutan.**
Thimphu: Central Statistical Office, Planning Commission, Royal Government of Bhutan, 1986- . annual.

This, the only book on the topic, is a handy and useful publication, with many statistical tables on different aspects of Bhutan's population and economy. Economic growth was estimated at an annual average of six per cent in the three years to March 1982, but the rate fell slightly in the year to March 1983, because of a reduction in revenue from forestry products; low rainfall in 1983-84 led to poor harvests and was expected to depress overall economic growth further.

315 **Strategies, approaches and systems in integrated watershed management.**
Rome: FAO, Forest Resources Division, 1986. 232p. (FAO conservation no. 14).

This book, which originated from an Expert Meeting on Strategies, Approaches and Systems in Integrated Watershed Management (2 Feb.–1 March 1985 in Kathmandu), provides information on economic aspects, training centres, research centres, watersheds, forestry, shifting cultivation of Bhutan, India, Indonesia, Nepal, the Philippines and Thailand.

316 **Supplementary resolutions adopted by the 54th session of the National Assembly held from 17 June to 27 June 1981.**
Thimphu: National Assembly of Bhutan, 1981. 10p.

This is a very important publication by the National Assembly which contains 35 resolutions concerning (1) salary for Gups (village headmen) and their clerks; (2) matters relating to inclusion of people's representatives under the Bhutan Civil Service Rules; (3) regarding drafting of rules for the selection of Gups; (4) matters relating to taxes; (5) life insurance scheme for the public; (6) stricter penalty for theft of antiques; (7) women in the police force for women criminals; (8) foreign labour in villages for the collection of resin; (9) distribution of law books concerning citizenship and inheritance tax; (10) regarding mortgage of ancestral house and land; (11) production of sureties during proceeding of court case; (12) anonymous letters of complaint should not be accepted; (13) matters relating to the military; (14) army recruitment from villages; (15) establishment of radio broadcasting station in Bhutan; (16) imparting training at agricultural demonstration farms; (17) introduction of teaching in regional languages in schools; (18) regarding facilities for school teachers and teacher-training programmes; (19) irrigation project at Gaylegphug; (20) drinking water supply scheme with aid from UNICEF; (21) facilities for disabled persons; (22) classification of Gung; (23) recruitment of labour for Dzongkhag works; (24) gobar (cow dung) gas plants; (25) matters relating to pasture land in Shemgang; (26) prevention of forest fires; (27) collection of firewood; (28) mining projects; (29) sale of cash crops; (30) aid to small business; (31) matters relating to Ministry of Foreign Affairs; (32) matters relating to water channels from southern Bhutan areas to nearby Indian villages; (33) presentation of livestock – Act and By-laws; (34) aid from the international fund for agricultural development; (35) Fifth Five-Year Plan (1981-86) for eight districts.

317 **Third Meeting of SARC Foreign Ministers, Thimphu.**
Kuensel, vol. 20, no. 17 (28 April 1985), p. 2-8.

The Foreign Ministers of seven South Asian countries (Bhutan, Bangladesh, India, Nepal, the Maldives, Pakistan and Sri Lanka) met in Thimphu on 13-14 May 1985. The text examines the achievements of the South Asian Association for Regional Co-operation (SAARC) since the first meeting of the Foreign Ministers in New Delhi in 1983, and stresses their collective resolve to strengthen mutual cooperation in order to promote economic cooperation, mutual trust, and understanding of each other's

Economy

problems. It also outlines the significance of the annual meetings, gives a brief history of the SAARC, and includes the joint communiqué issued at the conclusion of the conference.

318   **The least developed countries: introduction to the LDCs and to the Substantial New Programme of Action for them.**
United Nations Conference on Trade and Development.   New York: United Nations, 1985. 157p.

This book provides the text of the 'Substantial New Programme of Action for the Least Developed Countries', and covers topics such as: economic condition and development; gross domestic product; programmes of action; economic aid to least developed countries, such as Bhutan, Afghanistan, Bangladesh, the Maldives, Nepal and Samoa.

319   **South Asian co-operation in industry, energy and technology.**
Edited by Arif Abidali Waqif.   New Delhi: Sage, 1987. 259p.

These are the papers of a seminar on 'Regional cooperation for development of industrial and energy sectors in South Asia', held in Hyderabad, India in 1984. They evaluate the economic cooperation, resources development, technical, trade and scientific cooperation between Bangladesh, Bhutan and India.

320   **The road to Bhutan.**
Daniel Wolfstone, M. P. Gopalan.   *Far Eastern Economic Review*, vol. 44 (9 April 1964), p. 85-6.

Provides information on the First Five-Year Development Plan of Bhutan, formally launched in 1961. As financier and architect of the Plan, India provides most of Bhutan's economic requirements, but the outbreak of the Sino-Indian war in 1962 resulted in a slowing down of progress in Bhutan. The article also reveals India's efforts in building roads in Bhutan and in sponsoring it for membership of the Colombo Plan in 1962 and concludes that shortage of skilled personnel continues to be a serious impediment to Bhutan's economic and social progress.

321   **Workshop on the Evaluation and Planning of Human Resources Development (1985): Thimphu, Bhutan.**
Thimphu: Royal Government of Bhutan, United Nations Development Programme, 1985. 68p.

The workshop was organized by the Royal Civil Service Commission, the Government of Bhutan and the United Nations Development Programme to make the best use of human resources for the development of the country. The text here is the Report of the Workshop on the Evaluation and Planning of Human Resources Development, Thimphu, 27 May–2 June 1985.

Trade and Industry

322   Trade through the Himalayas: the early British attempts to open Tibet.
Schuyler Cammann.   Princeton, New Jersey: Princeton University
Press, 1951. 186p. bibliog.
This work deals with some little-known activities of the East India Company regarding
trans-Himalayan trade, and shows the eager, commercially minded diplomacy of the
eighteenth-century English company members. There are many pages on Bhutan
(24-9, 46-54, 63-7, 97-100, 105-6, 144-5) covering history, politics and trade missions.
The preliminaries to the Bhutan expedition of 1773 (p. 155-6), and the principal
articles of the treaty of peace with Bhutan in 1774 (p. 160-1), are also covered.

**323   On trade between Calcutta, Darjeeling, Bhootan and Tibet (and between
Assam, Tibet and West China).**
A. Campbell, H. Hopkinson.   *Journal of the Royal Society of Arts*,
vol. 17 (1869), p. 558-73.
After 1773 the British Parliament began to show increasing interest in the business
affairs of the East India Company and its territorial possessions in India. This is a
useful survey of the trade of the Company at the time of writing the article.

324   Cooch Behar and Bhutan in the context of Tibetan trade.
A. Deb.   *Kailash*, vol. 1, no. 1 (1973), p. 80-8.
The state of Cooch Behar was ceded by its ruler to India under the arrangement
known as the Cooch Behar Merger Agreement (28 August 1949). The state, whose
northern frontiers are about 20 miles south of the Bhutan range of hills, was merged
with West Bengal in January 1950. Parts of Cooch Behar, where the Bhutanese used to
trade, were part of Bhutan at that time. This article gives some general information on
the country, but primarily it is concerned with Bhutanese trade relations with Tibet
and China between 1772 and 1865. It also includes the British Government's views on
trade, and their interest in establishing trade links with Bhutan and Tibet. The author
also highlights the Chinese merchandise (including silk, gold, porcelain and tea) which
went to Bhutan.

Trade and Industry

325   **An enquiry into the silk industry in India. Report with appendices.**
Calcutta: Government of India, 1915. 3 vols.
Provides information about the production of silk in various states of India, together with new areas of silk production. Volume 1 gives information on the imports and exports of India to Nepal, Bhutan and Tibet. It covers the period 1904 to 1914.

326   **Information on trade and commerce of Bhutan at a glance.**
Thimphu: Trade and Information Centre, Department of Trade and Commerce, 1985. 195p.
This publication gives information on the statistics of Bhutan's foreign trade, broken down both by categories of goods and by trading partner. Since the 1960 ban on trade with Tibet, Bhutan's main trading partner has been India, although timber, locally produced spirits and cardomom are also exported to the Middle East and Western Europe.

327   **Of trade and transit.**
Economic and Political Weekly, vol. 13, no. 13 (1 April 1978), p. 563-4.
This article, by a special correspondent, is about trade and other relations between Bhutan and India. According to the 1949 treaty between the countries, Bhutan has always accepted India's guidance in its foreign affairs. Bhutan's trade was only with India, but in 1978 the Indian Government agreed that Bhutan could sell goods to Third World countries, if they were not needed by India. It was a significant departure from the trade relations which existed with India previously, and the article suggests that India should take the initiative to scrap the 1949 treaty with Bhutan and extend its friendship to Bhutan on equal terms.

328   **Some interesting documents.**
S. C. Sarkar.   *Bengal Past and Present*, vol. 44, no. 87-88 (July-Dec. 1932), p. 42-53.
Sarkar examines the interaction between Bengal's foreign trade and domestic policies and objectives. It is a useful survey of trade and commerce between Bengal, Bhutan and Tibet covering the period between 1769 and 1830. The 1778 trade agreement between the East India Company and Bhutan Lama – written in Bengali script – is also included.

329   **Some notes on the intercourse of Bengal with the northern countries in the second half of the eighteenth century.**
S. C. Sarkar.   *Indian Historical Records Commission Proceedings*, vol. 13 (Dec. 1930), p. 99-109.
The papers gathered together in this volume were originally read at thirteen meetings held in Patna. This particular paper provides information about the commercial interests of the British government with Tibet, Nepal and Bhutan. It is full of interesting details about the commercial intercourse between Bengal and the northern countries of Tibet, Nepal and Bhutan, and also shows a great eagerness on the part of the British authorities to expand trade with these countries. On the subject of

commerce treaties with Bhutan, the Treaty of April 1774 – at the end of the Cooch Behar campaign – promised to allow Bhutea caravans to visit Rangur (India) annually and free from any duties; it also reserved exclusively for the Bhuteas the trade in indigo, tobacco, animal skins dyed red, and betelnut.

Agriculture

330 **Bhutan – establishment of a veterinary diagnostic laboratory: project findings and recommendations.**
Rome: FAO, 1986. 29p.
The Food and Agriculture Organization of the United Nations undertakes many projects to help developing countries. This report is about setting up animal husbandry and veterinary services in Bhutan.

331 **Bhutan – forestry development: project findings and recommendations.**
Rome: Food and Agriculture Organization of the United Nations, 1983. 45p.
This was one of the first projects sponsored by the United Nations for the development and preservation of the forests in Bhutan. The main body of the report gives a summary of its findings and makes recommendations for agricultural training, and for forest management and development in Bhutan.

332 **Bhutan region to be developed with $4.75 million IFAD loan.**
Kuensel, vol. 21, no. 13 (30 March 1986), p. 3-4.
Bhutan is one of the world's least developed countries, has an average annual per capita income of only $120. Its topography imposes limitations on agriculture, with only 3 per cent of the land area under cultivation. It therefore comes into the group of countries to which the IFAD (International Fund for Agricultural Development) attaches high priority in extending its assistance. The loan aims to improve the agricultural production and livelihood of at least 40,000 farming families, and gives particular attention to women's involvement both in farming and in weaving activities. This is the second loan from IFAD to Bhutan. The first loan of $7.5 million (including a grant of $600,000), was approved in 1980 for small-farm development and an irrigation rehabilitation project.

333 **Agrarian relations in a hill region.**
Buddhadeb Chaudhuri.   In: *The Himalayas: profiles of modernisation and adaptation*, edited by S. K. Chaube.   New Delhi: Sterling, 1985, p. 91-112.

This article is based on the author's fieldwork conducted in the area from 1950 to 1981. The area studied is Kalimpong (West Bengal), which formerly belonged to Sikkim until it was conquered by Bhutan in 1706. After the war of 1865 it was annexed by the British, under the Senchulla Treaty of 11 November 1865. In the past, Lepchas and Bhutias were the only people living in the area, but in the early 20th century a large number of Nepalis migrated into the area. In 1981 Nepalis constituted about 80 per cent of the total population, and the rest of the population included Bhutias and Lepchas. The author has outlined the significant features of the development programme, cooperative farming, the agrarian structure, and a rural credit system which exists in the area.

334 **National plans for agricultural development in Asia-Pacific region: a compilation.**
Bangkok: FAO, 1987. 277p.

This book provides some very useful information on the planning of agricultural development in developing countries. These include Bhutan, Bangladesh, Burma, China, the Cook Islands, Fiji, India, Indonesia, the Republic of Korea, Malaysia, the Maldives, Nepal, Pakistan, the Philippines and Samoa.

335 **Project report on Forestry Training Institute (FTI) of Bhutan.**
Ernst Zeller.   Thimpu: Helvetas, 1986. 99p.

Zeller discusses the concept of forestry which was introduced quite recently into Bhutan. He reviews the forestry situation, and outlines the need for setting up training centres and training programmes for the development and preservation of forests in Bhutan.

Transport

336 **Bhutan – technical training in mechanized logging and road construction: project findings and recommendations.**
Rome: FAO, 1986. 25p.
This is another project on Bhutan by the United Nations Food and Agriculture Organization, concerned on this occasion with road construction and training centres for building roads.

337 **Lyonpo Jagar inaugurates Chirang–Dagapela Road.**
R. C. Gaylephug. *Kuensel*, vol. 15, no. 20 (18 May 1980), p. 3-4.
The Honourable Home Minister of Bhutan (Lyonpo Tamji Jagar) inaugurated the Damphy–Daga Road construction on 28 April 1980. The road, when completed, will connect Chirang and Dagapela region with Thimphu and Phuntsholing Highway, and its 85 kilometres will eventually be extended to Chimakothi in the west. The author discusses Bhutanese customs and ceremonies on such occasions, gives information on the cost of constructing the road, and discusses the people's cooperation in the road-building programme. The article concludes that the country is trying to mechanize the road construction programme in order to avoid the involvement of much manual labour.

Environment and Town Planning

338   **Physical planning in Bhutan: guidelines for the development of settlements.**
Bruno Hoesli.   Thimpu: Helvetas Consultants, 1985. 2nd ed. 73p.
This booklet covers the physical development plan for the urban areas of Bhutan. Although it looks a bit out of date, it is still a useful reference manual and includes a survey of land use and economic activity, together with specific development proposals.

339   **Bhutan's radical environmental policies.**
Geoffrey Lean.   In: *Bikas-Binas: development–destruction, the change in life and environment of the Himalaya*, edited by Kunda Dixit, Ludmilla Tuting, foreword by Christoph Von Furer-Haimendorf. Munich, West Germany: Geobuch, 1986, p. 71-9.
The book as a whole has many contributors from Asia and Europe and its aim is to discuss the links between ecology, development, and tourism. This particular chapter covers the physical environment and the agricultural and industrial pursuits of the people of Bhutan. The author discusses the fact that Bhutan does not follow the rest of the Himalayan people in destroying their forests. They have seen what has happened elsewhere once the trees have gone: the rains have stripped the top soil from the mountains and caused landslides, floods and subsequently failure of crops in the denuded fields. Only one per cent of the trees are cut each year in Bhutan, although the natural regeneration of the forest is two and a half times as great. And the trees that are cut are chosen on ecological rather than commercial grounds. This sort of approach is aimed at preserving both the country's culture and its environment, and is one of the pillars of Bhutan's development strategy. Also included are some comments on tourism, mountaineering, protecting Bhutan's culture from outside influence, and foreign aid which has no strings attached. This book is available from Ratna Book Distributors, Kathmandu, Nepal.

Environment and Town Planning

340 **Proceedings of the United Nations inter-regional seminar on the role of surveying, mapping and charting in country development programming.**
Ottawa: Department of Energy, Mines and Resources, 1985. 311p.

This seminar – which was held from 4 to 8 November 1985 in Aylmer, Quebec – provides information on: cartography, land development and planning, geography, information systems, maps, topography, remote sensing, economic development, technology transfer to developing countries (Bhutan, China, Nepal and Sri Lanka).

341 **Conservation of Asia's natural heritage: the planning and management of protected areas in the Indomalayan Realm.**
Edited by J. W. Thorsell. Gland, Switzerland: International Union for Conservation of Nature and Natural Resources (IUCN), 1985. 243p.

This book was the result of the 'International Union for Conservation of Nature and Natural Resources. Commission on National Parks and Protected Areas – working session, held on 4-8th February 1985'. It provides information on national parks and reserves, environmental protection and international cooperation on Asia – Bangladesh, Bhutan, India, Indonesia, Democratic Kampuchea, Malaysia, Nepal, Thailand and Vietnam.

342 **Towns in the mountains.**
Kathmandu: International Centre for Integrated Mountain Development, 1986. 31p. (ICIMOD phase 1 workshop series, no. 2).

The subjects covered in this pamphlet – based on the International Workshop on planned urbanisation and rural–urban linkages in the Hindu Kush–Himalaya Region, 25-29 March 1986 in Kathmandu – are: regional cooperation and development, rural–urban migration, urban planning, environmental aspects, and the socio-economic conditions of mountain areas – Bhutan, China, India, Pakistan and Nepal.

The Arts

General

343   **Thunder dragon textiles from Bhutan: the Bartholomew collection.**
Mark Bartholomew.   Kyoto, Japan: Shikosha, 1985. 125p.
Bartholomew provides an extremely useful work on the textiles of Bhutan. Textiles are considered by the Bhutanese to be their highest form of artistic expression. There are 72 colour plates in the text, offering the first major documentation of the art of weaving from the earliest to recent times. This book provides a unique guide to the culture and textile art of the country. The text of the book is in both English and Japanese.

344   **Vajrayana in art of Ladakh and Bhutan – some clues.**
Ronald M. Bernier.   *Himalayan Research Bulletin*, vol. 2, no. 3 (1982), p. 37-40.
These pages include a short introduction to the Vajrayana in the art of Ladakh and Bhutan. Vajrayana is a name given in Indian Buddhism to the last phase of development of the Mahayana Buddhism, of which Vajrayana is the continuation, although by its name it is designated as a separate 'Yana' or means to salvation.

345   **Linking intricate workmanship with dynamic feelings – handicrafts.**
Dorji Nyima.   *Asian Culture*, vol. 35 (Summer/Autumn 1983), p. 17-19.
This article is very useful to tourists who seek information on the handicrafts of Bhutan. It includes brief information on antiques, embroidery, sculpture, wood-carving, masks, metal-work, wood-turning, bamboo and cane crafts, textile products and hand-made paper. The places where the handicrafts are available are also mentioned.

346 **Nagapattinam and other Buddhist bronzes in the Madras Museum.**
   T. N. Ramachandran.   Madras: Government Press, 1954. 150p.
The author has made an elaborate study of about 350 Buddhist bronzes of the
Mahayana, which were discovered at the sites of viharas founded by the Shailendras of
Sumatra during the time of the Chola kings, Rajaraja I and Rajendra Chola I. Vihara
or Bihar (a state of India) is presumed to be the Sanskrit term for a Buddhist
monastery. Viharas were provided for the accommodation of Buddhist monks living
together in communities. Rajaraja I and Rajendra Chola I (1022-63 AD) were kings in
South India. These bronzes depict not only history but also the art of that time. This
illustrated volume includes 30 plates.

347 **Himalayan art: wall-painting and sculpture in Ladakh, Lahaul and**
   Spiti, the Siwalik ranges, Nepal, Sikkim and Bhutan.
   Madanjeet Singh.   London: Macmillan, 1968. 269p. bibliog.
This publication is the first of a new series in the 'Unesco Art Books' collection. The
author, a well-known writer of art books, illustrates themes characteristic of the
Himalayan culture and style of art. Its purpose is to relate the presentation of
significant, and generally little-known, works of art to the study and interpretation of
cultures. The art of the Himalaya is largely a religious art, which through the centuries
has expressed the faith and ideals of monks. The religion and art of the Himalaya are
derived from northern and central India and it remains closely allied to them. On the
subject of Bhutan (p. 255-84) the author provides a brief summary of the history of art,
accompanied by reproductions of photographs of Buddha, some Hindu deities,
monasteries, and birds. Bhutan's art history had a late start in about the 15th century
AD, and its artistic heritage is very rich and varied, as seen in the few examples of its
treasures reproduced here.

348 **Arts and crafts of Tibet and the Eastern Himalayas.**
   J. Claude White.   *Journal of the Royal Society of Arts*, vol. 58 (1910),
   p. 584-94.
A very useful general survey of Tibet, Bhutan, Nepal and Sikkim, this article includes
a general introduction to such arts and crafts as silverwork, wood-carving, and rug-
weaving. Appendix II is on the class and families of Bhutias, and appendix III lists the
names of the Lepcha families.

Painting and architecture

349 **Bhutanese architecture.**
   Philip Denwood.   *Asian Affairs*, vol. 58, New Series 2, pt. 1 (Feb.
   1971), p. 24-33.
Philip Denwood, Lecturer in Tibetan at the School of Oriental and African Studies,
London, spent a study year in Bhutan and Nepal in 1968, and this article is the result.
The author provides a brief history of Bhutan and Buddhism, and examines the
architecture which has been relatively untouched by modernization and preserves
many of the old Tibetan patterns. He argues that the techniques of house-building

The Arts. Painting and architecture

were learned from the Tibetans, but a simple comparison of constructional methods strongly suggests an origin to the west of Tibet, in the areas occupied in early historical times by speakers of Iranian languages. The techniques themselves go back to the remotest antiquity and seem to have been originally developed in the Middle East. There is also a short account of the technique of building, followed by plans of houses and some photographs of interesting buildings.

350 **Architecture in Bhutan and Ladakh.**
Corneille Jest, Joseph Allen Stein. In: *The Himalaya: aspects of change*, edited by J. S. Lall in association with A. D. Moddie. Delhi: Oxford University Press, 1981, p. 296-303.

The intention of this paper (chapter 18) is to make more widely known these unique and vital cultures, the survival of which is now endangered by easier access, tourism, and incipient industrialization. It is in fact a comparative and historical study of the architecture of Bhutan and Ladakh. In Bhutan the Dzong (part fort and part temple) is built on a commanding site in relation to the valley, and serves as the religious, administrative and social centre of the region. The walls of the buildings are massive and plain, logically made heavy at the base, rising upwards with decreasing thickness and increasing openness. There is heavy rainfall in Bhutan and earthern-walled structures are capped and protected by a sloping wooden roof which appears lightly perched over the building and provides protected storage for fuel and fodder. The work also provides information about the architecture of sacred and ceremonial buildings, temples, and ordinary houses in villages and towns.

351 **Auspicious symbols and luminous colours – art and architecture.**
Françoise Pommaret-Imaeda. *Asian Culture*, vol. 35 (Summer/Autumn 1983), p. 30-9.

This article starts with an introduction to the historical and religious background, including discussions on Bhutanese art, paintings and sculpture. The subjects of Bhutanese art are always religious: the Wheel of Life; the Four Guardians; the thousand Buddhas; Guru Rimpoche, and Buddhist sects. Paints are traditionally made from minerals and vegetables, and the colours are applied in a particular order associated with a symbolic meaning. Paintings and sculptures are executed by monks or laymen who work in special workshops. The disciples of a master do all the preliminary work while the fine work is executed by the master himself. This article also includes a brief survey of architectural forms in Bhutan. These are very diverse: chortens (stupas), temples, monasteries, fortresses, palaces, and village houses – all together these compose a landscape which is unique to Bhutan.

Music, dance and festivals

352 **'The admonition of the thunderbolt cannon-ball' and its place in the Bhutanese New Year.**
Michael Aris. *Bulletin of the School of Oriental and African Studies*, vol. 39, no. 3 (1976), p. 601-35.

This is a very interesting textual study of a document which is recited annually to an assembled militia organization during the New Year festival called 'Puna Dromcho' or 'Punakha Dromcho'. In 1408 Tsong-kha-pa, the great reformer of Tibetan Buddhism, introduced to Lhasa the New Year festival of the 'Great Prayer', and since 1644 the festival has been celebrated in Bhutan. It is a festival of national importance marking the transition from the old to the new year.

353 **Celestial praise of Guru Limpoche – Tshechu festivals.**
Yoshiro Imaeda. *Asian Culture*, vol. 35 (Summer/Autumn 1983), p. 20-30.

An examination and analysis of the Tshechu festival of Bhutan. Tshechu literally means 'Tenth Day' of the month. It is regarded as the most popular festival and is very colourful. The times and duration of the Tshechu vary from one region to another, but the festival always take place on the Tenth Day of the month. The festival is celebrated in honour of Padma Sambhava, an Indian saint, popularly known by the Bhutanese as Guru Rimpoche or Guru Limpoche. The Guru founded Nyingmapa (old school of Lamaism) about 800 AD and the school has still many followers in Bhutan. Guru Rimpoche is highlighted by the twelve episodes of his life which occurred on the tenth day of the month at different moments of his life. There is a brief summary account of each episode together with the ceremonies connected with it. The text is illustrated with beautiful colour photographs.

354 **Bhutanese New Year's celebrations.**
Robert and Beatrice Miller. *American Anthropologist*, vol. 58, no. 1 (Feb. 1956), p. 179-83.

The article provides a descriptive account of the New Year's celebrations in two Bhutanese towns (Pedong and Sakyong) from 26 to 30 December 1954. The observance is stated to have no religious significance, but to the Bhutanese of the area its importance far outweighs that of the later celebrations of the official and religious Tibetan New Year. The authors give a good description of the archery contests and dances which go with it. At the celebrations, the contests are usually between two different localities, and the most remarkable features of the celebrations in contrast to those of their neighbouring Sikkimese and Tibetan co-religionists, is the fact that religious symbolism seems to be at a minimum. The article concludes with a description of the big feast, which marks the end of celebrations; the cost of the food and beer provided is shared by all the archers.

355 **Tibetan Buddhist rites from the monasteries of Bhutan.**
New York: Lyrichord Discs, 1971.

This phonodisc (Lyrichord LLST 7255-58) of the music of Bhutan recorded by John Levy includes four booklets to go with the records. They are Vol. 1: Rituals of the Drukpa Order; Vol. 2: Sacred dances and rituals of the Nyingmapa and Drukpa

Orders; Vol. 3: Temple rituals and public ceremonies; and Vol. 4: Tibetan and Bhutanese instrumental and folk music.

356 **Tibetan music.**
London: School of Oriental and African Studies, University of London, 1967.
This tape of 8 reels holds music of Tibet recorded and produced by Philip Denwood, a Tibetan expert in the SOAS, University of London. It includes Bhutanese music on reel 3.

Folklore, customs and sports

357 **The life style and customs of the Bhutanese people.**
B. Chakravarti. In: *Family, marriage and social change on the Indian fringe*, edited by S. M. Dubey, P. K. Bordoloi, B. N. Borthakur.
New Delhi: Cosmo, 1980, p. 41-8.
The life and economy of the average Bhutanese centres around agriculture and animal husbandry. Because of the small scale of industrialization, the traditional life-style of the Bhutanese people is not likely to be changed in the near future. Chapter 3 covers their non-vegetarianism and drinking; marriage, polygamy, divorce and inheritance; the dress pattern of men, women, high officials, Lamas and ordinary people; and the patterns of house-building and animal husbandry.

358 **Spiritual living: enthusiastic enjoyment – daily life and entertainment.**
Rigzin Dorji. *Asian Culture*, vol. 35 (Summer/Autumn 1983), p. 8-16.
This article is an anthropological analysis of Bhutanese society as a balanced hierarchy which embraces both the social and natural orders, a situation which was made possible by the performance of rituals at home and in the monasteries of Bhutan. It contains very useful information about birth, marriage, sickness and death rituals; ceremonies relating to house construction; promotion of an individual; archery contests; and the observance of nine evil days of the year when people do not work, eat, drink, or perform good things such as marriage ceremonies.

359 **Ein Kapitel des Ta-se-sung.** (A chapter of the Ta-se-sung.)
Albert Grünwedel. In: *Festschrift für Adolf Bastian zu seinem 70 Geburtstage, 26 Juni 1896.* Berlin: Reimer, 1896, p. 461-82.
The author includes an excerpt in both the Tibetan and Lepcha languages from the Ta-se-sung, a collection of legends about the founder of Lamaism, Padma Sambhava. A glossary of useful words and illustrations are included in the article. Padma Sambhava was a native of northern India who established Mahayana Buddhism in Tibet, Bhutan, and the adjoining areas.

The Arts. Folklore, customs and sports

360 **Padmasambhava und Mandarava.**
Albert Grünwedel. *Zeitschrift der Deutsche morgenländische Gesellschaft*, vol. 52 (1898), p. 447-61.
The author discusses the history and legends about Padma Sambhava and his consort, Mandarava. He includes a selection from the legends in the Lepcha language, transliterated into Roman letters. A German translation is provided in the text. Padma Sambhava, an Indian saint, went to Tibet in 747 AD from Nalanda University at the invitation of Khri Srong, the then King of Tibet. He spread Mahayana Buddhism in Tibet, Bhutan, Sikkim, and the adjoining areas.

361 **Archery in Bhutan.**
Victor Rosner. *Anthropos*, vol. 62 (1967), p. 419-32.
Archery is one of the most important sports in Bhutan. Rosner provides a brief history, geography and religion of Bhutan, and this is followed by a complete treatise on archery. The equipment required for the sport, the clothes worn by the archers, and how the sport is played, are depicted with photographs alongside the text. In the olden days it used to be an essential requirement for kings, but nowadays any able-bodied man who has reached a certain proficiency in the sport, irrespective of rank or status, can take part in an archery contest. At more formal archery meetings, sponsored by the government, they also stage dances for distinguished guests attending the archery contest. The author describes in detail a dance which he saw in 1963 and concludes that archery will one day be relegated to a form of entertainment for distinguished guests in Bhutan. Like polo in India, it will be the sport of the few in Thimpu and Paro, but in remote villages of Bhutan it will remain as popular as before because the terrain will always exclude football and hockey, and lack of communication will preclude cinema as entertainment.

Mass Media

362   **Asian Recorder.**
   New Delhi: Recorder Press, 1955- . weekly.
A weekly digest of important developments in Asian countries, modelled after *Keesing's Contemporary Archives* (q.v.). It covers social, economic, political, educational, and cultural events, and includes excerpts from newspapers, magazines, press releases, and United Nations publications. There are quarterly, annual and triennial indexes. The *Recorder* is arranged alphabetically by country and within the country alphabetically by subject. It mentions items relevant to Bhutan.

363   **Facts on file: a world news digest, with cumulative index.**
   New York: Facts on File, Oct./Nov. 1940- . weekly. loose-leaf.
This publication has a cumulating twice-monthly index. There is a bound yearbook with five-year indexes. It is less detailed and more popular in style than *Keesing's* (q.v.).

364   **Indian Press Index.**
   Delhi: Delhi Library Association, 1968- . monthly.
This is a monthly index of about twenty-five leading English-language Indian newspapers. It contains author and area entries. A quarterly supplement gives all the book reviews published in the newspapers.

365   **Keesing's Contemporary Archives: weekly diary of world events.**
   Bristol, England: Keesing, 1 July 1931- . weekly. loose-leaf.
Summarizes British and foreign news, abstracted from news agencies' reports, official sources and the principal newspapers of each country. Sources are cited, but not always precise details of date and page. Speeches and texts of treaties, etc. may appear in full. There is a fortnightly cumulating index insert, which eventually becomes annual. Index entries are mainly under countries; subject indexing is less adequate. As

Mass Media

from 1959 maps are indexed under subjects as well as under 'maps'. It is a very useful index to anything significant occurring in Bhutan.

366   **Kuenphen Digest.**

   Phuntsholing, Tibet: Kuenphen Enterprise, 1982- . monthly.

This news magazine in English, edited by Karma Tenzin Dorji, is quite useful for local news.

367   **Kuenphen Tribune.**

   Phuntsholing, Tibet: Kuenphen Enterprise, 1982- . monthly.

This English news magazine, edited by Karma Tenzin Dorji, is based on the same style as the *Kuenphen Digest* (q.v.).

368   **Kuensel.**

   Thimphu: Department of Information, Ministry of Development,
   Royal Government of Bhutan, 1965- . weekly.

This is an official bulletin of the Royal Government giving news and current affairs about Bhutan. It is published in English, but issued also in Tibetan. It is the only newspaper in Bhutan, and its circulation in 1988 was about 12,500.

Professional Periodicals

369   **Asian Culture.**
Tokyo: Asian Culture Centre in Tokyo, 1972- . quarterly.
A quarterly newsletter in English which provides regular information by means of reports, essays and articles on various aspects of Asian culture as well as news about cultural activities generally, both in the region and at UNESCO. The idea of this newsletter is to strengthen ties among the peoples of Asia and between them and UNESCO. Articles on Bhutan appear from time to time.

370   **Asian Survey.**
Berkeley, California: University of California. 1961- . monthly.
This periodical covers the whole of Asia, and carries articles on historical, political and literary topics. In addition to occasional articles on a particular aspect of a country, a survey of the past year's events is carried regularly in one of the early issues of the following year.

371   **China Report.**
New Delhi: Centre for the Study of Developing Societies, 1964- . bi-monthly.
Articles, discussion papers, documents on contemporary China and Himalayan states are included. Features on Bhutan appear from time to time.

372   **Far Eastern Economic Review.**
Hong Kong: Review Publishing, 1946- . weekly.
This is a news journal which covers both South and South-east Asia, along with the Pacific rim. Some articles on Bhutan's politics and economic development appear in it from time to time. A summary of each year's events in the country is also included in the *Asia Yearbook* (q.v.) published annually by the same company.

373 **Himal.**
Kathmandu: Himal Associates, 1988- . bimonthly.
This news magazine covers the Himalayan region of Hindu Kush, Kashmir, Ladakh, Nepal, Tibet, Sikkim, Bhutan and the North East of India. It provides a non-specialist but intelligent reporting of development and ecological issues, including brief reviews of recent books.

374 **India Quarterly.**
New Delhi: Indian Council of World Affairs, 1945- . quarterly.
The main articles in this journal are generally highly specialized, with an emphasis on politics and international affairs, but it also includes a bibliography of Indian publications in the field of social sciences in every issue.

375 **Indo Asian Culture.**
New Delhi: Indian Council of Cultural Relations, 1952- . quarterly.
The journal is sponsored by the Indian Council of Cultural Relations and publishes articles on Indian and Asian culture, on both contemporary and past issues.

376 **International Studies.**
New Delhi: Indian School of International Studies, 1959- . quarterly.
This journal always publishes scholarly articles in the field of international politics, economics and law. It also includes an annual bibliography on Indian and world affairs, and there is a survey of recent research in each issue.

377 **Journal of Asian Studies.**
Ann Arbor, Michigan: Asian Studies Association, 1922- . quarterly.
The journal, which was entitled *Far Eastern Quarterly* until 1956, is published by the Asian Studies Association for scholars interested in Asia, and carries articles principally on historical, political, anthropological and literary topics, as well as book reviews. The Association's annual *Bibliography of Asian Studies* was included in the journal until 1979, but is now published separately.

378 **Journal of Indian History.**
Kerala, India: University of Kerala, 1921- . three issues a year.
The Department of History, University of Kerala, Trivandrum is concerned with promoting scholarly activity, especially relating to Indian history. Its journal carries articles on political, social, cultural and intellectual life in India. All the major specialists in Indian history, both Indian and foreign, are represented here. Some articles on Bhutan also appear in it.

379 **Tibetan Review.**
Dharamsala, India: Sheja, 1965- . monthly.
Tibetan Review is a monthly publication of news and features on Tibet and the Tibetans. Besides a regular survey of the current situation in Tibet, based on refugee statements and other reliable sources, the paper reports on the activities of the free

Tibetans living in exile in India, Bhutan, Sikkim and Nepal. Each issue contains articles of general interest on various aspects of Tibetan life and culture. The paper also seeks to provide a forum for free and frank discussion on the question of Tibet and the various problems of the Tibetan people.

Yearbooks, Encyclopaedias and Directories

380 **Asia Yearbook.**
Hong Kong: Far Eastern Economic Review, 1960- . annual.
This publication was formerly known as *Far Eastern Economic Review Yearbook*. A general overview is followed by an alphabetical country-by-country analysis of politics, social affairs, foreign relations, and economic conditions. Bhutan is usually included.

381 **Countries of the world and their leaders yearbook.**
Detroit, Michigan: Gale Research Company, 1981- . annual.
This yearbook has background notes on 168 countries, each with a map, and includes the Central Intelligence Agency's list of 'Chiefs of State and Cabinet members of foreign governments'. Each annual has about 4 pages of information on Bhutan's people, geography, government, growth rate, history, economy, political conditions, principal government officials, foreign relations, and travel notes for people who want to visit Bhutan.

382 **Directory of trade promotion/developing organizations of developing countries and areas in Asia and the Pacific.**
Bangkok: Economic and Social Commission for Asia and the Pacific (ESCAP). Technical Co-operation Division, 1983. 100p.
This booklet provides some general information on trade promotion organizations dealing with Afghanistan, Bhutan, China, the Cook Islands, Hong Kong, India, Indonesia, Malaysia, the Philippines, the Republic of Korea, Samoa, Singapore, Sri Lanka and Thailand.

383 **Europa yearbook, 1986: a world survey.**
London: Europa Publications, 1986. 27th ed. 2 vols.
This includes both an introduction and statistical survey of each country. On Bhutan, it provides up-to-date information on its history, geography, languages, religion, flag, government, defence, economic affairs, transport, social welfare, education, tourism,

public holidays, weights and measures, and the currency and exchange rates. Volume 2 includes an index to regions. Each edition of the yearbook has about two pages of information on Bhutan.

384 Indian Year Book of International Affairs.
Madras, India: University of Madras, 1952- . annual.
This interesting annual includes articles on various aspects of international affairs and law. It is published under the auspices of the Indian Study Group of International Affairs at the University of Madras.

385 Encyclopaedia of Buddhism.
G. P. Malalasekera.   Colombo: Government of Ceylon. 1961- .
Four volumes have been published so far. The entire work will comprise about 15,000 pages and contain information on all aspects of Buddhism. Scholars from all over the world are contributing articles to the encyclopaedia. It is a very useful major reference work.

386 The Statesman's Year-book: statistical and historical annual of the states of the world for the year 1989-1990.
Edited by John Paxton.   London: Macmillan, 1989. 126th ed. 1691p.
This annual has background notes on 168 countries, each with a map, and includes the Central Intelligence Agency's list of Chiefs of State and Cabinet members. On Bhutan, it provides information on its history, area, population, climate, reigning king, history of government, defence, international relations, economy, banking, energy and natural resources, industry, trade, tourism, communications (roads, post, broadcasting, newspaper), justice, religion, education, welfare, and information on the diplomatic official of Bhutan to the UN. The yearbook was first published in 1864.

387 Cambridge encyclopaedia of India, Pakistan, Bangladesh, Sri Lanka, Nepal, Bhutan and the Maldives.
Edited by Francis Robinson.   Cambridge: Cambridge University Press, 1989. 520p. maps. bibliog.
This volume is a good attempt to study South Asia in one volume. It covers the land, people, history, politics, foreign relations, economics, religions, society and culture. Today more than one out of five members of the human race lives in South Asia. About 69 scholars from universities and research institutes in the USA, the UK, South Asia and Australia have contributed to it. Pages 161-4 are an introduction to Bhutan's internal development and foreign relations up to 1952. These pages also include a list of rulers of Bhutan from 1724 to 1952. Pages 231-2 and 239-40 are about the politics of Bhutan from 1907 to the mid-1970s, together with a list of Kings and Prime Ministers of Bhutan from 1926 to date. Information on Bhutan is scattered, but it is useful book for the general reader.

388 An almanack for the year of Our Lord.
Joseph Whitaker.   London: Whitaker, 1868- . annual. maps.
This is an annual publication with a sub-title 'containing an account of astronomical and other phenomena and a vast amount of information respecting the government, finances, population, commerce, and the general statistics of the various nations of the

Yearbooks, Encyclopaedias and Directories

world, with an index containing nearly 20,000 references'. Each issue covers Bhutan with a brief account of its history, government, the King of Bhutan, Council of Ministers, population, trade and imports and exports with UK. It is usually known as the 'Whitaker's Almanack'. The year 1989 saw the 121st edition of this work.

Bibliographies

389 **Asian bibliography.**
Bangkok: UN Economic Commission for Asia and the Far East,
Library, 1952- . semi-annual.
This is a selective list of the ECAFE Library's book accessions dealing with Asia and
the Far East. Titles of publications in the Asian languages have been translated. About
500 items per issue on 35 areas (A–Z) with subject sub-divisions (e.g. Bhutan:
Agriculture – Administration etc.). The Bhutan section is a good guide to the most
significant works acquired by the Library. The bibliography has author, title and area
indexes.

390 **The Himalayas: a classified social scientific bibliography.**
Asok Basu. Calcutta: K. P. Bagchi, [1984?]. 318p.
There are 4,417 entries in this work, arranged according to the Dewey Decimal
Classification scheme. Each entry is marked with a serial number for retrieval
purposes. It lists about 272 entries on Bhutan (Sr. No. 2629–2901), and most of the
publications (periodical articles, books, pamphlets, and newspaper articles) date from
the 19th century to 1983.

391 **Guide to Indian periodical literature.**
Gurgaon, India: Prabhu Book Services, 1964- . quarterly.
The guide is an author–subject index to articles and other reading material appearing
in about 500 Indian journals in the fields of social sciences and humanities. The entries
are arranged alphabetically, and each entry has an author and subject entry except
where there is no author. Library of Congress subject headings are used and each issue
includes a list of the periodicals indexed. This publication is more or less on the lines of
Wilson's *Social Sciences and Humanities Index*.

392 **Bibliography of the Himalaya.**

R. K. Gupta. Gurgaon, India: Indian Documentation Service, 1981.

This bibliography contains 4,772 entries, mostly of a technical nature. The entries are arranged alphabetically by author, under the following subjects: bibliography; general accounts of travels; physical geography and geomorphology; climate; geomorphology and water resources; mineralogy, geochemistry and geophysics; petrology; human geography; plant resources; animal resources; and soil conservation.

393 **Historical abstracts: bibliography of the world's periodical literature.**

Santa Barbara, California: American Bibliographical Center – Clio Press, 1955- . quarterly.

Original coverage: 1775-1945; 2 parts. as from vol. 17 (Spring 1971): A. 'Modern history abstracts, 1775-1945'; B. 'Twentieth century abstracts, 1914-1970'. Scope expanded in 1973 to cover the period 1450 to the present day. As from 1980 the bibliography is in 2 volumes – Vol. 1, to contain abstracts and references published between 1973-78; Vol. 2, to cover 1979 material and also give citations to books and dissertations. It is useful for some references on Bhutan.

394 **South Asia.**

Cecil Hobbs. *Quarterly Journal of the Library of Congress*, vol. 26, no. 2 (1969), p. 117-20.

At the time of writing, the author was an employee of the Orientalia Division of the Library of Congress. He discusses national and other significant bibliographies for Bhutan, Ceylon, India, Nepal, Pakistan, Sikkim and Tibet. Of these at that time, only India had a national biography, but at present most of the countries except Bhutan have them.

395 **Indian National Bibliography.**

Calcutta: Central Reference Library, Ministry of Education, October-December 1957, and from 1958- (in progress).

This is an authoritative bibliographical record of current Indian publications in English and in Indian languages. It records material received by the National Library in Calcutta, under the Delivery of Books and Newspapers Act of 1954, as amended in 1956. It was previously issued quarterly with annual cumulation, an alphabetical subject index being included with every issue, but since 1968 it has been issued monthly, and covers all publications except musical scores, maps, periodicals and newspapers (except the first issue under a new title), keys and guides and other ephemeral material. The arrangement is by Dewey Decimal Classification number. Entries of books in Indian languages and Tibetan are transliterated into Roman script, with diacritical marks. There are author, title and subject indexes with every issue.

396 **A guide to source materials in the India Office Library and Records for the history of Tibet, Sikkim and Bhutan 1765-1950.**

Amar Kaur Jasbir Singh. London: British Library, 1988. 187p.

This is a bibliographical guide to the archival material in the India Office Library and Records (now a part of the British Library). The source material, both official and private, which documents the development of British India's political relations with the Himalayan states is most essential for the study of their history. Most of these records came to an end with the independence of India in 1947, and for information about the period after that it is necessary to go to the records of the Commonwealth Relations Office and the Foreign Office in order to study the British policy towards these states. This is the first guide available on the subject, and it is hoped that it will stimulate fresh investigations of the unique material described in it.

397 Library of Congress accessions list – India.
New Delhi: American Libraries Book Procurement Center, 1962-80. Vols 1-19. monthly.
This lists publications from India purchased by the Library of Congress on its own behalf and for other American libraries and institutions. Each December issue includes a cumulative list of serials and indexes for the whole year. Items published in each language are arranged in separate alphabetical sequences.

398 Library of Congress accessions list – South Asia.
New Delhi: Library of Congress Office, 1981- . monthly.
This list is a successor to the earlier separate country lists. It includes titles from Afghanistan, Bangladesh, Bhutan, India, the Maldives, Nepal, Pakistan, and Sri Lanka. The entries are organized by the country of publication. Under each country the entries are divided into sections for monographs, special materials, and serials. In the monograph sections, entries are sub-divided by the language of publication, and within each language, listed in alphabetical sequence. Each of the two sections which list special materials and serials is arranged in a single alphabetical sequence, without regard to language. Author, title and subject indexes are included in the monthly issues; annual cumulations of each are issued as part 2 of the December issue. Serial supplements are published periodically, cumulating all new serial titles, changes, and deletions listed in preceding monthly issues.

399 List of books, articles, etc., on Assam – supplementary to that made on Sikkim and Bhutan.
Compiled under the direction of the Librarian, Imperial Library, Calcutta. Calcutta: Imperial Library, 1904. 11p.
Books on Bhutan covering the British period and treaties between the two countries.

400 A guide to manuscripts and documents in the British Isles relating to South and South East Asia. Vol. 1. London.
J. D. Pearson. London: Mansell, 1989. 319p.
This supplement to Wainwright and Matthews (q.v.) contains the resources held by 93 libraries and institutions. Unlike its predecessor, this volume contains a summary list of the resources held by the India Office Library and Records. There are a few references to Bhutan.

401 Buddhism: a select bibliography.
Satyaprakash. Gurgaon, India: Indian Documentation Service, 1976. 172p.
This bibliography indexes 2,565 articles, research papers, book reviews, and other significant materials on all aspects of Buddhism published in 84 Indian journals. There

are, in addition, 450 book titles. The entries have been classified and arranged by author and subject in alphabetical sequence. A second edition was published in 1986.

402 **Sikkim 1800-1968: an annotated bibliography.**
Linda G. Schappert.   Honolulu, Hawaii: East-West Center Library, University of Hawaii, 1968. 69p. (Occasional paper no. 10.)

This bibliography lists the holdings of libraries in the Boston area, especially those of the Harvard University Library system, on Sikkim, her history, culture and natural resources. Since Bhutan's history was closely tied with that of Great Britain, India, Bengal, Assam, Tibet, Nepal and Sikkim, much of the material on Bhutan will be found by pursuing these subjects in the bibliography. Books, periodical articles, and other material which relates in part to Bhutan are cited.

403 **A guide to western manuscripts and documents in the British Isles relating to South and South East Asia.**
Compiled by M. D. Wainwright and Noel Matthews under the general supervision of J. D. Pearson.   London: Oxford University Press, 1965. 532p.

This guide includes manuscripts and documents in both private and public collections, including national and university libraries, county record offices and regimental museums. Resources in the India Office Library and Records, London, are excluded from this guide. There are a few references to Bhutan.

Index

The index is a single alphabetical sequence of authors (personal and corporate), titles of publications and subjects. Index entries refer both to the main items and to other works mentioned in the notes to each item. Title entries are in italics. Numeration refers to the items as numbered.

India and the China crisis 248
India and Tibet: a history of the relations which have subsisted between the two countries from the time of Warren Hastings to 1910; with a particular account of the mission to Lhasa of 1904 138
India: a handbook of travel 52
India Office Library and Records, London 113, 396, 400
India: official standard names approved by the United States Board on Geographic Names 39
India Quarterly 374
Indian Alps, and how we crossed them; being a narrative of two years residence in the Eastern Himalaya and two months tour into the interior, by a Lady Pioneer 64
Indian Council of Cultural Relations 375
Indian Frontier Administrative Service 227
Indian National Bibliography 395
Indian Press Index 364
Indian Study Group of International Affairs, Madras University 384
Indian Year Book of International Affairs 384
India's aid diplomacy in the Third World 288
India's foreign policy: selected speeches [Nehru], September 1946-April 1961 268
India's Northern security (including China, Nepal and Bhutan) 103, 236
India's role in the

emergence of contemporary Bhutan 136
India's wildlife and wildlife reserves 87
Indigo 329
Indira 71
Indo-Aryan languages 155
Indo Asian Culture 375
Indo-Chinese border dispute 17, 220, 238-9, 248, 250-5, 257, 260-3, 267, 285
Indo-gangetic plain 79
Indo-Nepalese war (1793-1816) 121
Indonesia 18, 312, 315, 334, 341, 382
Industry 12, 19, 214, 290-1, 303, 319, 322-9, 386
Infrastructure 293, 305
Information on trade and commerce of Bhutan at a glance 326
Inlow, E. Burke 6
International Association of Buddhist Studies 191
International Court of Justice 15
International Fund for Agricultural Development 332
International Institute for Environment and Development, London 305
International Studies 376
International Union for Conservation of Nature and Natural Resources 341
Introduction to Mahayana Buddhism with especial reference to Chinese and Japanese phrases 192
Introduction to tantric Buddhism 180
Iranian people 349
Irrigation 303, 316, 332
Ispahani, M. Z. 249
Israel–Palestine conflict 231

IUCN see International Union for Conservation of Nature and Natural Resources
Ives, J. D. 303

J

Jackson, M. D. R. 54-5
Jad Bhotias 211
Jain, R. K. 250
Jambey 230
Jambudwipa: a blueprint for a South Asian community 283
Jangpangi, B. S. 24
Japan 63, 69, 192, 198, 299, 312
Jasbar Singh, A. K. 121, 396
Jäschke, H. A. 162, 172
Jataka or stories of the Buddha's former births 179
Jelep La Pass 58
Jenkins W. M. 27
Jest, C. 350
Jhansi 76
Jhingran, A. G. 24
Jigme Dorje Wangchuck [Wangchuk] 11
Jigme Dorjee [Dorji] 230, 257
assassinated (1964) 97, 230, 276
Jigme Singye Wangchuck [Wangchuk] 93, 101, 128, 133, 141, 209, 247
Johar Valley Bhotias 211
John Marshall in India: notes and observations in Bengal, 1668-1672 63
Journal of Asian Studies 377
Journal of Indian History 378
Journal of travels in Assam, Burma, Bootan, Afghanistan and the neighbouring countries 59

123

World War II 266

Map of Bhutan

This map shows the more important towns and other features.

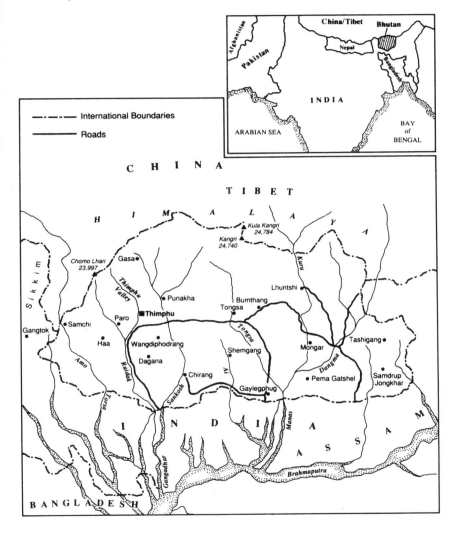